U.S. Submarines in World War II

U.S. Submarines in World War II
An Illustrated History

Larry Kimmett
Margaret Regis

Navigator Publishing • Seattle, Washington

Acknowledgments

This history is confined to the Pacific Theater where almost all U.S. submarines fought and all credited sinkings by U.S. subs took place. Representative patrols and actions appear in chronological order to illustrate the development of the undersea war and the gradual dominance U.S. submarines achieved over Japanese sea-lanes. We have used the statistics compiled after the war by the Joint Army-Navy Assessment Committee (JANAC) as our basic source on Japanese ship sinkings. Although this compilation is known to have many individual errors, and may underestimate total sinkings, it gives approximate numbers for Japanese losses. We hope to update these figures as better information from Japanese archives becomes available. We regret that space limitations and the great scope of the Pacific naval war prevented the inclusion of many famous submarines, deserving captains, and noteworthy actions. Finally, we wish to thank the following individuals and organizations for their generous assistance in the preparation of this book:

Robert Lee Banister, Kollmorgen Corporation
Russell Booth, USS *Pampanito*
Patrick Britt
Slade D. Cutter (USS *Seahorse*)
Tudor Davis (USS *Halibut*)
Jeanne Eisen and the Naze family
John Fankhauser (USS *Porpoise*)
Paul Farace, USS *Cod*
E. C. Finney, Jr., Naval Historical Center
Frank R. Fisher (USS *Seahorse*)
William Galvani, Naval Undersea Museum
Carol Gibbens
Dennis Gobets
Charles R. Haberlein, Jr., Naval Historical Center
Dan Hagedorn, Smithsonian Institution
Roger Hubbard
Paul Kemp, Imperial War Museum
Joan Kloster, Manitowoc Maritime Museum
Sue Lemmon, Mare Island Naval Shipyard
B. E. Lewellen (USS *Torsk*)
Frank McGrane, Naval Undersea Museum
Pete Mitchell (USS *Flying Fish*)
National Security Agency
USS *Nautilus* Submarine Force Library and Museum
Richard O'Kane, USN ret. (USS *Tang*)
Fred Pernell, National Archives
Joe J. Phenneger (USS *Kingfish*)
George Rocek (USS *Sculpin*)
April Ryan
Steve Schapiro
Ervin O. Schmidt (USS *Torsk*)
Aldona Sendzikas, USS *Bowfin* Submarine Museum and Park
Stan Shockey
Roman Schweizer III
William Soczek (USS *Growler*)
Charles E. Stewart (USS *R-6*)
Mary Beth Straight, United States Naval Institute
Dan Sweet, United States Naval Base, Seattle
Mary Jo Valdes, USS *Bowfin* Submarine Museum and Park
Ralph Van Horn (USS *Flasher*)
Sally Van Natta
Jack C. Weiser, Time-Life
Kim Williams, USS *Bowfin* Submarine Museum and Park

Navigator Publishing
P.O. Box 1289
Kingston, WA 98346

Printed in the United States of America.

Library of Congress Cataloging-in-Publication Data

Kimmett, Larry.
   U.S. submarines in World War II: an illustrated history/Larry Kimmett, Margaret Regis.
      p.   cm.
   Includes bibliographical references and index.
   ISBN 1-879932-03-2 (hard cover).—ISBN 1-879932-01-6 (paper)
   1. World War, 1939-1945—Naval operations—Submarine. 2. World War, 1939–1945—Naval operations, American. 3. World War, 1939–1945—Campaigns—Pacific Area. I. Regis, Margaret, 1957– II. Title.
D783.K56 1996
940.54'51—dc20   95-49376

Cover art by April Ryan
Title page illustration: Gato-class fleet submarine

Contents

Old men forget; yet all shall be forgot,
But he'll remember, with advantages,
What feats he did that day. Then shall our names,
Familiar in his mouth as household words. . .
Be in their flowing cups freshly rememb'red.

SHAKESPEARE, *HENRY V*

Introduction

On December 7, 1941 the successful Japanese attack on the U.S. battle fleet at Pearl Harbor heralded a twin revolution in naval warfare. The sunken battleships along Ford Island announced that the aircraft carrier had replaced the battleship as the major offensive weapon of surface fleets. It was less obvious as the first U.S. submarines slipped out of Pearl Harbor to challenge the enemy's complete mastery of the Western Pacific, that these small ships would also play a pivotal role in Japan's defeat. Prewar naval doctrine called for submarines to serve in a subordinate capacity as scouts for the battle fleet, but Pearl Harbor and the rapid Japanese expansion forced them to become solitary commerce raiders. Operating all over the Pacific during the next four years, they sank a major part of the Japanese merchant marine and much of the Imperial Navy. Costs were high. The United States lost 52 submarines during the war—37 of them with all hands. One out of five American submariners in World War II never came back. Nevertheless, by the end of the war U.S. submarines completely cut the supply lines to an island nation, a feat that German U-boats failed to do in two world wars.

Tautog (above) returns home in 1945. The submarine began the war at Pearl Harbor on December 7, 1941, where its machine gunners shot down a Japanese torpedo plane headed for Battleship Row. It ended the war with 26 confirmed Japanese ships sunk—making *Tautog* the U.S. Navy's top scoring submarine of World War II.

The Japanese Empire

The arrival of an American Fleet under Commodore Matthew Perry in 1853 forced Japan to end its centuries-old isolation. Fearful of conquest by other European powers, a reformed Japan set out in the 1860s to turn itself into a first-class industrial and military power. Unfortunately, its new rulers copied the imperialist politics of the era and began a rapid expansion at the expense of neighboring countries. The Japanese fought a successful war against China in 1894 and acquired Korea and Formosa. In 1905, they astounded the world by defeating Russia in a naval and land war, and by "leasing" large areas of Manchuria from the prostrate Chinese government. These policies brought Japan into diplomatic conflict with the United States, which continually advocated an "Open Door" trading policy with China for all nations.

During World War I, Japan sided with Great Britain against Germany and enjoyed tremendous economic growth, selling war materials to the Allies. The boom ended with the arrival of the Great Depression in the late 1920s, and soon widespread poverty and destitution led to the rise of ultra-nationalist "salvation" movements. These groups, centered in the Imperial Army, believed only the expansion of the Empire could save the country from ruin.

In 1931, Japan's Kwantung Army defied the weak central government in Tokyo and conquered all of Manchuria. Ignoring international protests, the Japanese set up a puppet state called Manchukuo, and in 1937 invaded the rest of China. They seized the largest Chinese cities, forcing Chiang Kai-shek's government to retreat into the interior. Despite unparalleled ferocity against the Chinese people, the war settled into a costly stalemate.

Hirohito, the Emperor of Japan (top), reviews his troops during the Chinese war. On ascending to the throne in 1926, Emperor Hirohito designated his reign "Showa" or "Enlightened Peace." However, only political turmoil, world war, and defeat awaited Japan.

Japanese troops (above) shout *"Banzai"* (lit. "10,000 years") to celebrate an early victory in China. The Imperial Army's euphoria soon ended when troop commitments reached a million men, casualties rose, and costs exceeded five million dollars per day.

10

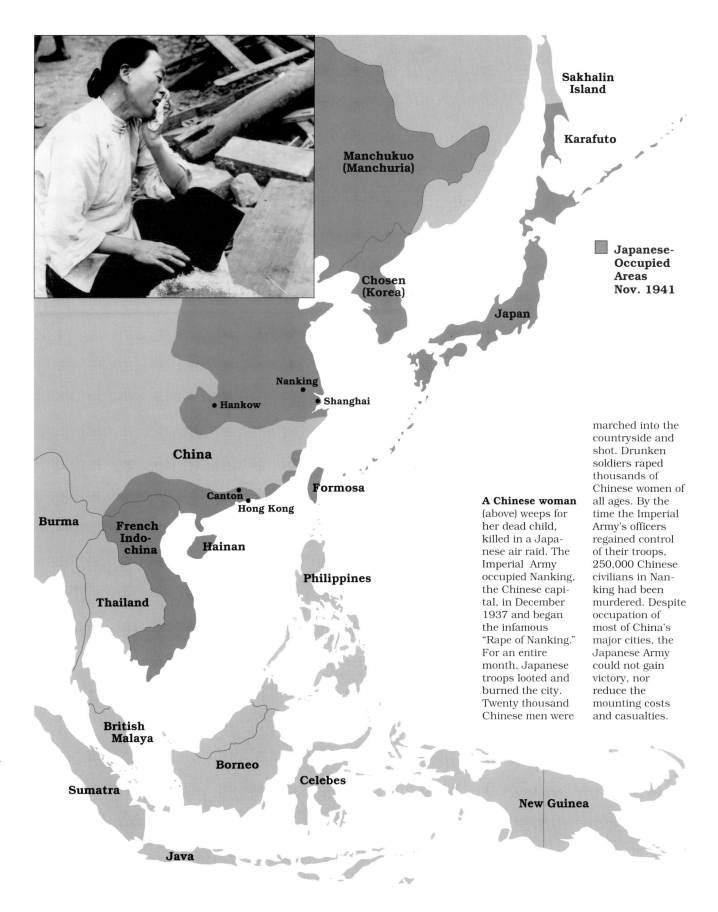

Sakhalin Island

Karafuto

Manchukuo (Manchuria)

Chosen (Korea)

Japan

Japanese-Occupied Areas Nov. 1941

Nanking

• **Hankow**   • **Shanghai**

China

Formosa

Canton •

Hong Kong •

Burma

French Indo-china

Hainan

Philippines

Thailand

British Malaya

Borneo

Celebes

New Guinea

Sumatra

Java

A Chinese woman (above) weeps for her dead child, killed in a Japanese air raid. The Imperial Army occupied Nanking, the Chinese capital, in December 1937 and began the infamous "Rape of Nanking." For an entire month, Japanese troops looted and burned the city. Twenty thousand Chinese men were marched into the countryside and shot. Drunken soldiers raped thousands of Chinese women of all ages. By the time the Imperial Army's officers regained control of their troops, 250,000 Chinese civilians in Nanking had been murdered. Despite occupation of most of China's major cities, the Japanese Army could not gain victory, nor reduce the mounting costs and casualties.

Two Plans

Japanese troops (left) attack Shanghai, China. The Imperial Army assigned 11 of Japan's 51 divisions, a total of 350,000 men, to the Southern Operation.

U.S.S.R.

Sakhalin Island

Manchuria

Korea

Japan

China

Bonin Islands

Formosa

Burma

French Indo-china

Hainan

Marianas Islands

Saipan

Thailand

Philippines

Caroline Islands

Palau

Truk

British Malaya

Borneo

Celebes

New Guinea

Solomon Islands

Sumatra

Java

Dutch East Indies

Australia

In the summer of 1941 Japan took advantage of France's defeat by Nazi Germany and occupied French Indochina. The United States, Britain, and the Netherlands immediately retaliated by cutting off oil sales to Japan. Desperate, the Japanese, who had no other source of petroleum, decided to launch the Southern Operation—a vast war plan to seize and hold Burma, the Philippines, Malaya, and the oil-rich Dutch East Indies. With the resources from these territories Japan could complete the conquest of China and establish an impregnable defense line around its new Co-Prosperity Sphere.

In the crucial action of the Southern Operation invasion, Japan's six largest aircraft carriers, escorted by a powerful surface fleet, would launch a surprise air raid on the main U.S. naval base in the Pacific at Pearl Harbor, Hawaii. Three hundred and sixty aircraft would smash the three carriers and seven battleships of the U.S. Pacific Fleet and open the path to Japan's conquest of East Asia.

Alaska
U.S.A.

Midway

Hawaii

Wake

Marshall
Islands

Kwajalein

Tarawa

Fiji

Japan's rapid rise as an industrial and military power, and its aggressive policies toward China early in the twentieth century, alarmed the United States Navy and set it to work on a plan to defeat Japan if war should come. American fears worsened after World War I when the League of Nations awarded Japan the strategic former German possessions of the Marianas, Caroline, and Marshall islands.

The U.S. Navy's war plan, code-named Orange (Orange = Japan), expected the Japanese to attack the Philippines to keep the United States from interfering in an invasion of China and Southeast Asia. War Plan Orange called for the U.S. Navy to maintain control of the eastern Pacific and, after amassing reinforcements over a two-year period, fight its way back through the Marshall, Caroline, and Marianas islands to retake the Philippines. There, the U.S. fleet would destroy the Japanese Navy in a climactic battle. An American blockade and bombing campaign would then compel Japan to surrender.

U.S. battleships (right) sortie on a prewar training mission. Although Japan and the United States had about the same battleship strength in the Pacific in 1941, the Imperial Navy had ten aircraft carriers to the U.S. Navy's three.

13

Early U.S. Submarines

On October 12, 1900 the U.S. Navy commissioned its first submarine, the USS *Holland*. Named in honor of its brilliant Irish-American inventor, John P. Holland, the sub combined an efficient gasoline-powered engine for surface running with a battery-powered motor for underwater propulsion. USS *Holland* proved such a success that the Navy ordered seven more submarines.

By 1911 Holland's corporation, the Electric Boat Company, delivered its first diesel-powered submarine, the *Skipjack*. The Navy gave command of the new boat to Lt. Chester W. Nimitz who would one day assume command of the U.S. Pacific Fleet.

World War I accelerated defense needs and the Navy ordered 100 new submarines. These included several experimental designs and 51 S-class boats. Although intended for coastal patrols, the 800 ton S-boats served as the main interwar U.S. submarine and won a number of victories in the Pacific at the beginning of World War II.

John P. Holland (above) stands in the conning tower of his submarine, USS *Holland*. He died in 1914 just after the outbreak of World War I.

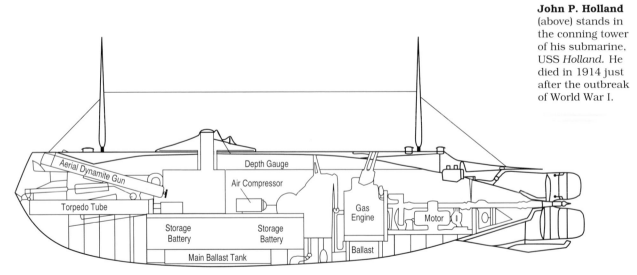

The USS *Holland* (SS-1) was launched in 1898. It was 53 feet 10 inches long and displaced 64 tons on the surface and 74 tons submerged. Its armament consisted of one 18-inch torpedo tube, three torpedoes, and one 8-inch pneumatic dynamite gun. The submarine carried a crew of seven and could dive to a depth of 100 feet.

Evolution of the U.S. Submarine

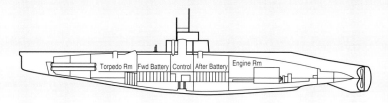

1917

L-class submarine Length: 165 feet; Displacement: 456 tons; Weapons: four 18-inch torpedo tubes and one three-inch deck gun; Speed: 14 knots surfaced, 10 knots submerged; Diving Depth: 200 feet; Crew: 28 men. Following World War I, the Navy built the slightly larger O- and R-class coastal defense submarines.

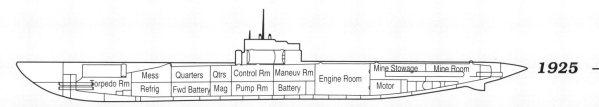

1920

S-class submarine Length: 211 feet; Displacement: 854 tons; Weapons: four 21-inch torpedo tubes, one four-inch deck gun; Speed: 14 knots surfaced, 11 knots submerged; Diving Depth: 200 feet; Crew: 42 men.

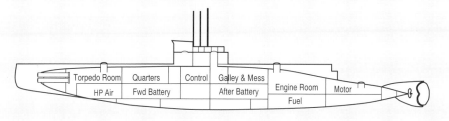

1925

V-4 submarine: Length: 381 feet; Displacement: 2,700 tons; Weapons: four forward 21-inch torpedo tubes, two stern torpedo tubes, two six-inch deck guns; Speed: 15 knots surfaced, 8 knots submerged; Diving Depth: 300 feet; Crew: 86 men. The Navy named the V-4 submarine *Argonaut* in 1931. *Argonaut* was the largest American submarine in commission during World War II and the only specially designed minelaying submarine built for the U.S. Navy. It could launch eight mines in ten minutes.

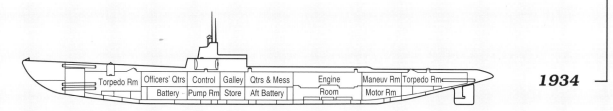

1934

Porpoise class submarine: Length: 301 feet; Displacement: 1,310 tons; Weapons: four forward 21-inch torpedo tubes, two stern torpedo tubes, one three-inch deck gun; Speed: 18 knots surfaced, 8 knots submerged; Diving Depth: 250 feet; Crew: 50 men. These were the last riveted hull submarines the U.S. Navy built.

Diagrams not to scale

Fleet Submarine

The U.S. Navy's efforts to produce a fleet submarine capable of fighting across the Pacific Ocean's vast distances led to the Gato-class design just before World War II. The Gato-class submarine was 312 feet long, displaced 1,526 tons surfaced, and could operate to a depth of 300 feet. The boat carried provisions for up to 75 days and enough fuel to cruise 11,000 miles on the surface at an economical 10 knots.

Manned by a crew of about 75 in wartime, the submarine carried 24 torpedoes and either a three-inch or four-inch deck gun. On the surface, four powerful diesel engines charged generators which could drive the ship's electric motors to a speed of 20 knots. When the boat submerged, two very large storage batteries provided enough power to move the submarine at nine knots for an hour or for 48 hours at a much slower two-knot speed.

Starting at the bow, the submarine's pressure hull was divided into nine watertight sections. First came the forward torpedo room with six loaded torpedo tubes, spare torpedoes, and bunks for a quarter of the crew. A watertight door opened into the the officers' quarters and ward room just above the forward battery space. The lower compartment enclosed 126 battery cells—enough to supply half the submarine's electrical power when submerged.

The next watertight door led to the control room. Here was the machinery for diving and surfacing the boat, as well as the switchboard and radio room. A hatch over the control room went up into the conning tower. This was the ship's combat center; it contained the periscopes, torpedo data computer (TDC), radar, and navigational plot.

A crewman leaving the control room passed above the after battery space and through the crew's galley and a bunk area for 36 men. Next came the forward and

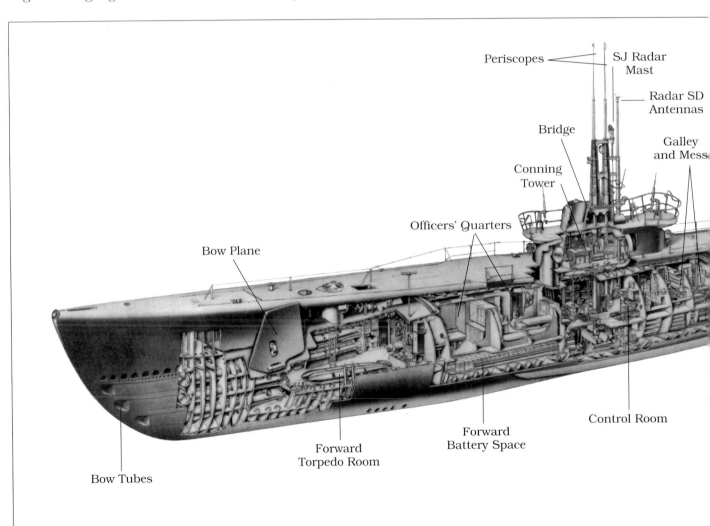

Periscopes — SJ Radar Mast

Radar SD Antennas

Bridge

Galley and Mess

Conning Tower

Officers' Quarters

Bow Plane

Control Room

Forward Battery Space

Forward Torpedo Room

Bow Tubes

after engine rooms. Two 1,600 horsepower diesel engines in each room lined the narrow walkway. Beneath these two compartments, four 1,100-kilowatt generators powered the main motors and charged the batteries.

Just aft of the generators, four electric motors turned the boat's twin propellors. Above the motor room, the maneuvering compartment's controls could change the submarine's speed or switch from diesel power to batteries. Last came the after torpedo room with four stern torpedo tubes. With this formidable machine the U.S. Navy attacked Japan's maritime empire.

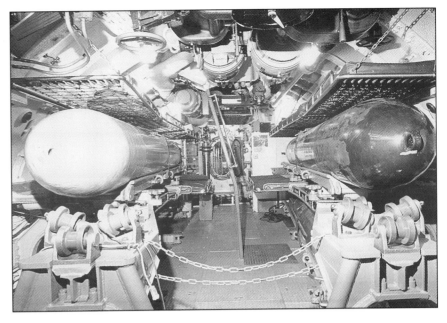

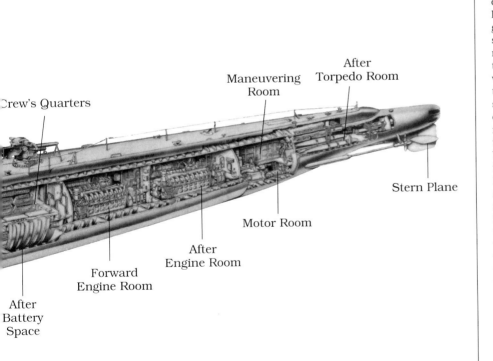

The fleet submarine (left) presented a small silhouette. It was designed to have a low center of gravity (to keep it stable) and was normally two-thirds submerged when riding on the surface. The superstructure deck, called the main deck, extended from the bow to just before the stern. Limber holes in the sides allowed sea water to enter all the hollow spaces in the superstructure and the deck when diving and to drain off when the submarine surfaced. Amidships, the conning tower stood above the main deck. It included a shielded area called the bridge, as well as the periscopes, radio compass loop, and radar antennas. Lookout perches were welded onto the upper periscope shears with a hoop to prevent seamen from being tossed overboard in rough weather. The after section of the deck held a four-inch deck gun for surface fighting.

The forward torpedo room (above) held sixteen Mark 14 torpedoes, each 20 feet long and weighing over a ton and a half. The fully-armed torpedoes had to be periodically checked or "routined" to insure successful operation during battle. Every week torpedomen lubricated the propellers, fins, and rudder of each torpedo before filling its high-pressure air flask to the required 2,800 pounds. Removing the torpedoes from the tubes, making the adjustments, and replacing them was a strenuous effort that took many hours.

Crew's Quarters

Maneuvering Room

After Torpedo Room

Stern Plane

Motor Room

After Engine Room

Forward Engine Room

After Battery Space

Fleet Submarine

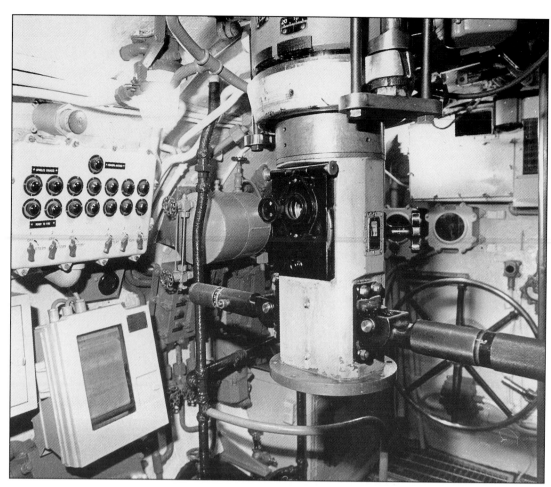

The periscope (left) was designed for high- and low-power observation. It had a telemeter which the captain used to estimate the range of an enemy vessel.

The captain's stateroom (bottom left) was large enough for one man. It consisted of a bunk, small desk with phone, and locked cabinet. The commander could monitor the boat's location with the depth gage and compass mounted behind the bunk.

The control room (bottom right) had a panel of red and green lights called the "Christmas tree" board. It signaled when the boat was watertight and ready to dive.

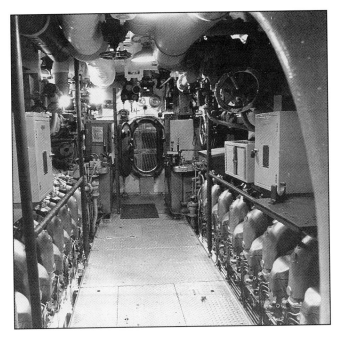

The after engine room (top left) housed the No. 3 and No. 4 main diesel engines and the main generators. It also held an auxiliary diesel engine and generator below the platform deck.

The maneuvering room (top right) held the controls to regulate electric current between the batteries, generators, and motors. The instruments also could alter the boat's speed, and switch power between the engines and batteries.

The after torpedo room (left), the last compartment on the submarine, contained four torpeodo tubes and four spare torpedoes. It also held the escape and rescue hatch (sealed in wartime), the stern plane tilting mechanism, and bunks for fifteen crewmen.

Aboard the Boat

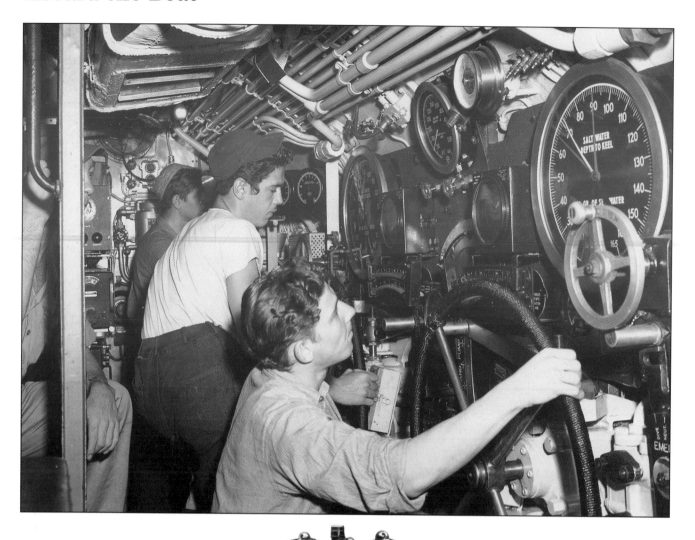

Submarines are among the most complicated machines ever built. To sail and fight such a ship requires a crew of specialists. Submarine pay was higher because of the danger. All crewmen were volunteers; no one was drafted to the submarine service. Each crewman had to pass strict written and oral examinations on all machinery in the boat to win his "dolphins" and be allowed to stay in the submarine branch.

A typical crew aboard a fleet boat consisted of 70 enlisted men with five to seven officers. Half of the crew were machinists, electricians, and torpedomen, while quartermasters (who kept logs), cooks, gunner's mates, radiomen,

a pharmacist's mate, a yeoman, and unrated firemen and seamen made up the rest. The senior chief petty officer who handled the enlisted men's affairs was known as the "chief of the boat."

The crew divided into three working sections to run the ship at sea. Each group stood watch at their duty stations four hours on and then took eight hours off. All hands followed this routine except the captain who was always on call. While on duty, the crew ran the ship's machinery, stood lookout, and did routine maintenance. Off duty, sailors slept in

one of the 36 bunks in the main crew's quarters, or in others rigged in the torpedo rooms. If awake they talked, read, studied for their qualifying exams, played cards, ate meals reputed to be the best in the Navy, and drank coffee.

The captain, the senior officer, directed this fighting warship. Usually, he was an Annapolis graduate about 35 years old with the rank of lieutenant commander. He was assisted by an executive officer who handled much of the boat's administration and helped him during attacks. The other three to five officers divided up responsibilities such as engineering, communications, and torpedo-gunnery.

20

Crewmen in the control room (top opposite) watch the gages and operate the hydraulic-powered handwheels which control the tilt of the bow and stern planes. The angle of the planes determines whether the submarine dives or rises.

The Dolphin Insignia (center opposite) was the coveted badge which showed

that a sailor had passed rigorous written and oral tests on the operation of all the submarine's systems and was therefore "qualified" as a submariner and eligible for higher pay.

The ward room (top left), in the officers' quarters, located above the forward battery compartment, served as officers' dining room,

meeting area, and conference room. Here, officers could prepare the many reports and records the Navy required during a war patrol.

In the galley (top right), a six-by-eleven kitchen located above the after battery compartment, the ship's cooks prepared coffee, snacks and three meals a day for 75 officers and men.

The forward torpedo room (left) not only served as home for the 20-foot-long, 3,400 pound Mark 14 torpedoes, but also held fifteen bunks for tired, off-duty sailors. The top bunks were considered most desirable because they gave their owners the most privacy. Crewmen sat on the middle bunks even while sailors used them for sleeping. The occupants of the lowest bunks were vulnerable to unintentional kicks and bumps.

The enlisted men's mess (above), located over the after battery compartment, had four tables and eight benches, and could feed 24 sailors at a sitting. The food, said to be the best in the Navy, was a necessary perk for men confined for weeks. When not in use as a dining room, it was the off-duty crew's 24-hour meeting center. Here, the men talked, drank coffee, played acey-deucey, listened to music and relaxed.

Pearl Harbor

On Sunday December 7, 1941, the morning the Japanese attacked Pearl Harbor, only four of the 21 submarines attached to the U.S. Pacific Fleet were in port. Three of them—*Dolphin, Narwhal,* and *Tautog*—were tied up at the submarine base on the harbor's East Loch, while the fourth, *Cachalot,* was in the Navy Yard for overhaul.

At 7:55 a.m. Japanese bombs exploded on Ford Island Naval Air Station, signaling the beginning of the air raid on Pearl Harbor. This brought the submariners to general quarters. Aboard the *Tautog,* the relief duty officer, Lt. William Sieglaff, ordered his men to break into the locked ammunition room and set up a .50 caliber machine gun on the deck. Twenty-four Japanese torpedo planes, on their way to Battleship Row, flew past the submarines at an altitude of 100 feet. The submarines opened fire and *Tautog* shot down one Japanese Kate bomber.

By 10 a.m. the attack was over. All four submarines had escaped damage, although *Cachalot* had one casualty—a sailor who was wounded in a strafing run. Fortunately, no bombs hit the submarine base, the sub tender USS *Pelias,* the adjacent Kuahua ammunition dumps, or the oil tank farms which held 140 million gallons of diesel oil.

The next day five more submarines—*Gudgeon, Thresher, Plunger, Pompano,* and *Pollack*—made it into Pearl Harbor despite attacks by nervous U.S. forces. With the seven serviceable submarines (*Cachalot* and *Narwhal* needed extensive repairs), Rear Admiral Thomas Withers began to carry out the urgent orders he received from Washington at 4 p.m. on December 7th: "Execute unrestricted air and submarine warfare against Japan."

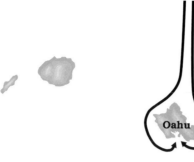

Hawaiian Islands December 7, 1941

Oahu

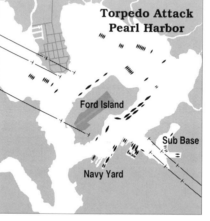

Torpedo Attack Pearl Harbor

Ford Island

Sub Base

Navy Yard

In the early morning of December 7, 1941 a Japanese task force of 31 ships, including six aircraft carriers, arrived at a point 230 miles north of Oahu. Just after 6 a.m. the carriers launched 353 planes in two waves to bomb the U.S. Pacific Fleet at Pearl Harbor. Approaching the anchorage at 7:53 a.m., Lieutenant Commander Mitsuo Fuchida gave his *Tora, Tora, Tora* (Tiger, Tiger, Tiger) attack order and sent the bombers, torpedo planes, and dive-bombers of the first wave down onto the unsuspecting American ships.

The U.S. Navy submarine base (below) at Pearl Harbor in 1941. Oil storage tanks and ammunition depots are seen behind the base.

Sailors from the submarine *Narwhal* (left) fire rifles and machine guns at Japanese planes during the attack. The bombers completely missed the submarine base even though it held the Fleet Headquarters building, machine shops, torpedo plant, docks, supply stores, training facilities, and housing for 2,500 men. This mistake proved costly for the Japanese Empire. U.S. submarines operating from Pearl Harbor sank over 112 Japanese ships in the year following the attack.

A captured Japanese photograph (above) of the torpedo attack on Battleship Row. A tremendous column of water rises from a torpedo hit on the battleship USS *Oklahoma.* Altogether, the Japanese raiders sank five out of the eight U.S. battleships in the harbor and seriously damaged or sank thirteen other ships. They also destroyed 165 aircraft at the island's six air bases, killed 2,403 Americans, and wounded another 1,178 personnel.

First Empire Patrol

On Thursday morning December 11, 1941 a hastily provisioned USS *Gudgeon* threaded its way down the debris-filled channel of Pearl Harbor and put to sea. The ship's destination was the southern entrance to the Inland Sea, where it would conduct the first offensive U.S. submarine patrol in Japanese home waters.

Gudgeon proceeded on the surface until Christmas day when it reached a point 1,500 miles from Japan where enemy air patrols were expected. Thereafter, in order to avoid detection, the submarine submerged in the daytime and traveled at full speed on the surface at night.

Twenty-one days after leaving Pearl Harbor *Gudgeon* arrived off Bungo Suido, the strait between Kyushu and Shikoku. Much to the surprise of Lieutenant Commander E.W. Grenfell there was little sea traffic, and navigational lights on shore were still lit. Over the next 12 days *Gudgeon* sighted six ships and made two attacks with probable damage to one Japanese freighter.

Calculating another three weeks for the return voyage, Grenfell departed the area on January 14th. Meanwhile, radio direction finders at Pearl Harbor located the Japanese submarine *I-73* passing Midway and ordered *Gudgeon* to intercept. *I–73* had participated in the Pearl Harbor attack by making a reconnaissance of Lahaina anchorage off Maui. It subsequently conducted a war patrol in Hawaiian waters.

At 9 a.m. on January 27th, the submerged *Gudgeon* picked up the sound of fast screws from a Japanese submarine on the port bow. Grenfell took three quick observations and fired three torpedoes. Two hit, and the enemy submarine vanished. *I-73* was the first warship ever sunk by an American submarine.

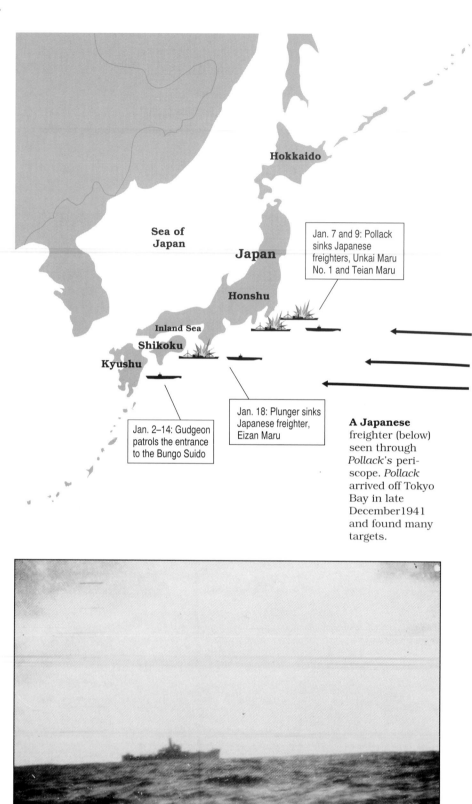

Jan. 7 and 9: Pollack sinks Japanese freighters, Unkai Maru No. 1 and Teian Maru

Jan. 2–14: Gudgeon patrols the entrance to the Bungo Suido

Jan. 18: Plunger sinks Japanese freighter, Eizan Maru

A Japanese freighter (below) seen through *Pollack*'s periscope. *Pollack* arrived off Tokyo Bay in late December 1941 and found many targets.

First War Patrols to Japan
Dec. 1941–Jan. 1942

In the first hectic days after the Pearl Harbor attack, Rear Admiral Thomas Withers, Commander Submarines Pacific Fleet, determined that seven of the nine submarines available at Pearl Harbor could be readied for war patrols quickly. He sent four subs to reconnoiter the Japanese-mandated Marshall Islands where the Navy feared another attack on Hawaii might be in preparation. The remaining three submarines, *Gudgeon, Pollack,* and *Plunger* were ordered on "Empire patrol" off the eastern coast of Japan. *Pollack* left Pearl Harbor on December 13th and arrived off Tokyo Bay on December 30th. In ten days *Pollack* made six attacks and sank two freighters: *Unkai Maru No. 1* and *Teian Maru.* The submarine *Plunger* left Pearl on December 14th and arrived off the northern entrance to the Inland Sea on January 4th. Although *Plunger* carried the new SD radar, a destroyer detected the sub early in the patrol and subjected it to severe depth-charging. *Plunger* escaped this attack and on January 18th sank the 4,700 ton cargo ship, *Eizan Maru.*

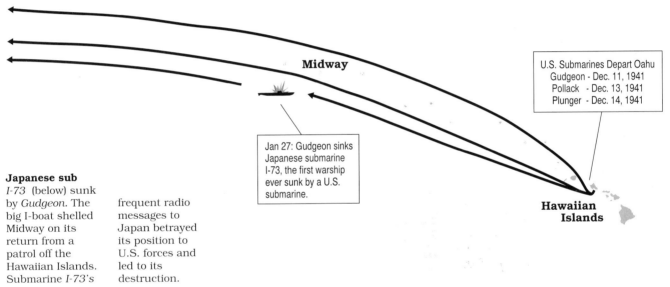

Midway

U.S. Submarines Depart Oahu
Gudgeon - Dec. 11, 1941
Pollack - Dec. 13, 1941
Plunger - Dec. 14, 1941

Jan 27: Gudgeon sinks Japanese submarine I-73, the first warship ever sunk by a U.S. submarine.

Hawaiian Islands

Japanese sub
I-73 (below) sunk by *Gudgeon.* The big I-boat shelled Midway on its return from a patrol off the Hawaiian Islands. Submarine *I-73's* frequent radio messages to Japan betrayed its position to U.S. forces and led to its destruction.

Philippine Disaster—Cavite

Just before noon on December 8, 1941 Japanese bombers destroyed half of the U.S. Army Air Force on the ground at Clark Field, north of Manila, and seized air superiority over the Philippines. The commander of the U.S. Asiatic Fleet, Admiral Thomas Hart, had planned to operate 29 submarines and three sub tender support ships from the Manila area, but the destruction of American air power opened Manila Bay to attack.

Two days later, at 1 p.m. on December 10th, 54 Japanese twin-engined planes of the 11th Naval Air Fleet on Formosa bombed Cavite Navy Yard. Fifty-two escorting Zero fighters brushed aside the few available U.S. interceptors. Despite the air raid warnings, more than 500 Philippine dock workers died in the explosions and hundreds were wounded.

Two bombs hit and sank the submarine *Sealion* and damaged the adjacent submarine *Seadragon*. The blasts killed five sailors, the first fatalities for American submarines in World War II. *Pigeon*, a small rescue ship, braved exploding ammunition near the wharf and towed *Seadragon* into the safety of the channel.

Heroic salvage efforts patched up *Seadragon*, but Cavite was completely destroyed. Faced with the immediate danger of further air attacks, Admiral Hart ordered the sub tenders *Holland* and *Otus* south to Java, and left the old tender *Canopus* camouflaged in Manila Bay to service the submarines for as long as possible. Twenty-two of the remaining 28 U.S. submarines fanned out around the Philippines to intercept the expected Japanese invasion. Hart ordered them to stay on patrol until food and fuel ran low, and then retreat to Java.

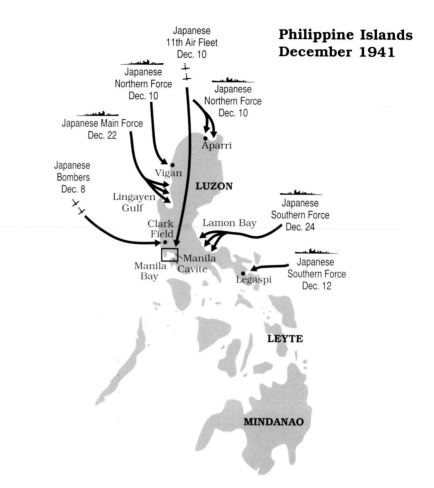

Philippine Islands December 1941

Japanese 11th Air Fleet Dec. 10

Japanese Northern Force Dec. 10

Japanese Northern Force Dec. 10

Japanese Main Force Dec. 22

Aparri

Japanese Bombers Dec. 8

Vigan

LUZON

Lingayen Gulf

Clark Field

Lamon Bay

Japanese Southern Force Dec. 24

Manila Bay

Manila Cavite

Japanese Southern Force Dec. 12

Legaspi

LEYTE

MINDANAO

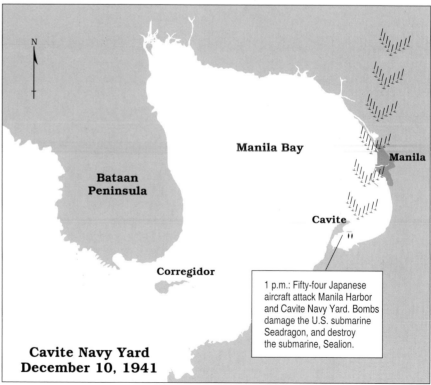

N

Manila Bay

Bataan Peninsula

Manila

Cavite

Corregidor

1 p.m.: Fifty-four Japanese aircraft attack Manila Harbor and Cavite Navy Yard. Bombs damage the U.S. submarine Seadragon, and destroy the submarine, Sealion.

Cavite Navy Yard December 10, 1941

Aerial view of Cavite Navy Yard (left). On November 27, 1941, the commander of the U.S. Asiatic Fleet, Admiral Thomas Hart, received a war warning from the Chief of Naval Operations to "expect an aggressive move by Japan within the next few days." Admiral Hart immediately sent his surface forces—three cruisers and 13 destroyers—to the southern Philippines, beyond the range of Japanese aircraft from Formosa.

Cavite Navy Yard on fire (above). Japanese bombs blew up Cavite's docks, oil tanks, radio station, and storehouses. Direct hits on the torpedo repair shop detonated dozens of U.S. torpedoes and added to the general destruction. The loss of 233 torpedoes— about 60 percent of the total supply—created a torpedo shortage for the Asiatic submarine force that would last through most of 1942.

27

Philippine Disaster—Lingayen Gulf

After the destruction of Cavite, Capt. John Wilkes, Acting Commander of U.S. Asiatic Submarines, spread his boats all around the Philippines in a thin, defensive perimeter. This formation disregarded the U.S. Army's conviction that the Japanese would land at Lingayen Gulf and march down Luzon's broad, hundred-mile plain to seize Manila.

Late in the afternoon of December 21, 1941, 73 transports, escorted by cruisers and destroyers, ferried 43,000 men of Japan's 48th Infantry Division toward the Lingayen beaches. Wilkes sent seven submarines—five fleet subs and two older S-boats—to attack, but it was too late. Only submarine *S-38* evaded the tight destroyer screen at the mouth of Lingayen Gulf and sank *Hayo Maru,* a 5,400 ton freighter. The Japanese consolidated the beachhead and sent a column south toward Manila.

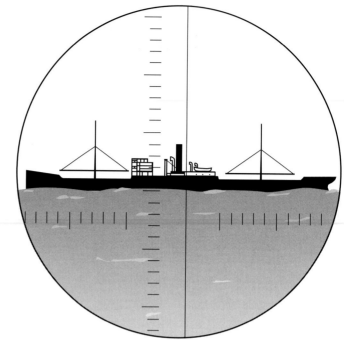

Hayo Maru
(above) pictured in *S-38's* periscope. The 5,400 ton transport was 20 years old, 400 feet long, and had a crew of 48. It was one of the 1,700 merchantmen vital to Japan's war machine and commerce.

Submarine *S-38*
(below) was almost twenty years old in 1941. By the standard of the newer fleet boats, *S-38* was primitive and hard to operate, but its sixteen Mark 10 torpedoes made it a dangerous weapon.

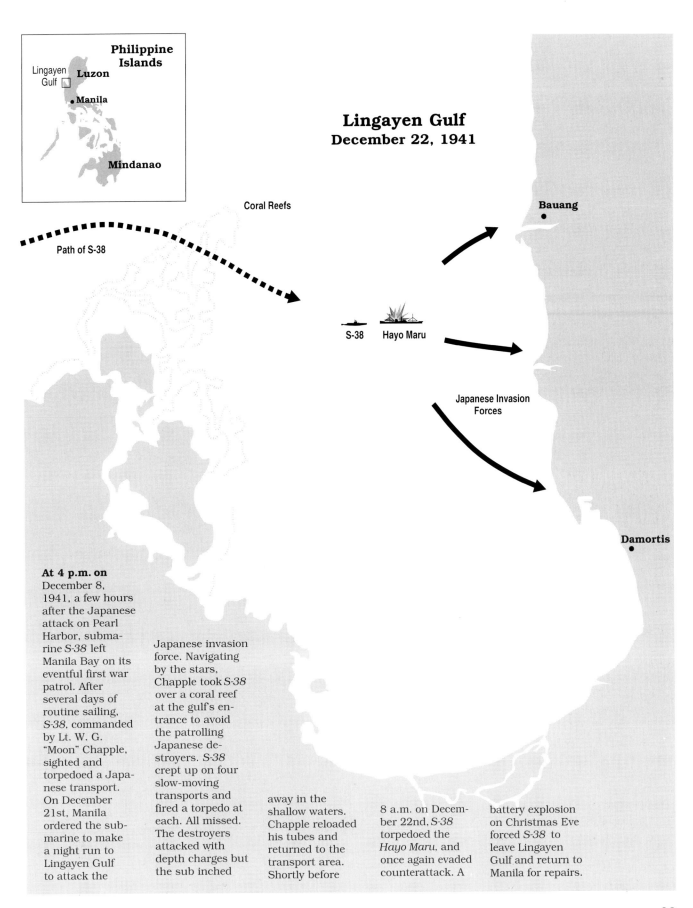

Philippine Islands

Lingayen Gulf
Luzon

• Manila

Mindanao

Lingayen Gulf
December 22, 1941

Coral Reefs

Path of S-38

Bauang
•

S-38   Hayo Maru

Japanese Invasion
Forces

Damortis
•

At 4 p.m. on December 8, 1941, a few hours after the Japanese attack on Pearl Harbor, submarine *S-38* left Manila Bay on its eventful first war patrol. After several days of routine sailing, *S-38*, commanded by Lt. W. G. "Moon" Chapple, sighted and torpedoed a Japanese transport. On December 21st, Manila ordered the submarine to make a night run to Lingayen Gulf to attack the Japanese invasion force. Navigating by the stars, Chapple took *S-38* over a coral reef at the gulf's entrance to avoid the patrolling Japanese destroyers. *S-38* crept up on four slow-moving transports and fired a torpedo at each. All missed. The destroyers attacked with depth charges but the sub inched away in the shallow waters. Chapple reloaded his tubes and returned to the transport area. Shortly before 8 a.m. on December 22nd, *S-38* torpedoed the *Hayo Maru*, and once again evaded counterattack. A battery explosion on Christmas Eve forced *S-38* to leave Lingayen Gulf and return to Manila for repairs.

Torpedo Failure

Mark 14 Torpedo

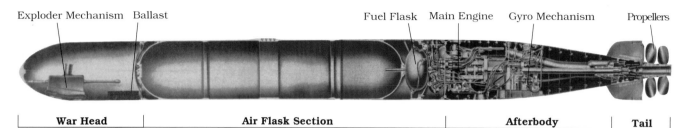

Exploder Mechanism Ballast Fuel Flask Main Engine Gyro Mechanism Propellers

War Head | Air Flask Section | Afterbody | Tail

The failure of U.S. subs to stop the Japanese invasion convoy at Lingayen Gulf doomed American control of the Philippines. Virtually all of the Imperial army used to conquer the islands arrived on the December 21st convoy. The Japanese captured Manila January 1st, and U.S. forces retreated to the fortified Bataan Peninsula.

The onslaught of war revealed many deficiencies in the submarine force: crews were not conditioned for extended patrols and maintenance was not up-to-date on the boats. Prewar tactical training overemphasized the dangers from aircraft and sonar-equipped destroyers, and discouraged night surface attacks. This doctrine made captains overcautious and narrowed their attacks to the limited range of submerged submarines.

None of these problems however, matched the unexpected operational failure of the Mark 14 torpedo. This weapon—just over 20 feet long with a 643 pound warhead—carried a secret magnetic exploder designed to detonate under a ship's keel. Unfortunately, due to stringent prewar economies, it had only been tested one time. In 45 separate attacks during the last weeks of December 1941, U.S. Asiatic submarines saw their Mark 14 torpedoes run under the target, explode prematurely, or hit the enemy ship without detonating. Ninety-six torpedoes were fired and only three Japanese ships sunk.

In August 1942 after dozens of complaints from submarine captains, the U.S Navy's Bureau of Ordnance admitted the Mark 14 torpedo ran ten feet too deep due to an improperly designed depth mechanism. The report also issued instructions for correcting the defect.

The shape of a vessel's magnetic field varied according to its location. Near the equator, the field flattened out to the shape of a disk. The exploder detonated when it first sensed the extended magnetic field—often before it reached the target. Magnetic exploders were disconnected in 1943.

Torpedoes struck the target but didn't explode. The spring-operated firing pin on the Mark 14 contact exploder often jammed in its guides during collision. This prevented it from reaching the fulminate cap to detonate the torpedo. A lighter firing pin solved this problem.

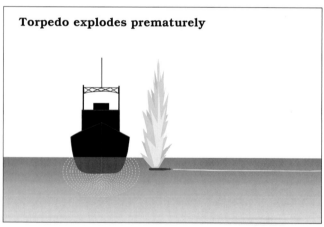

Torpedo runs too deep

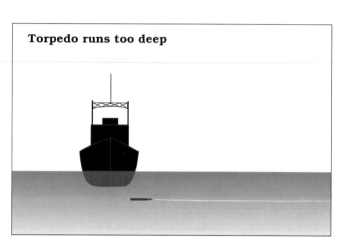

Torpedo explodes prematurely

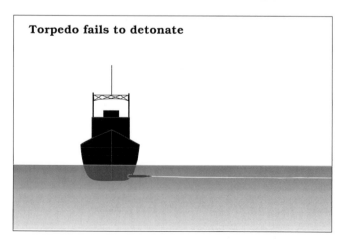

Torpedo fails to detonate

Mark 6 Magnetic Exploder Mechanism

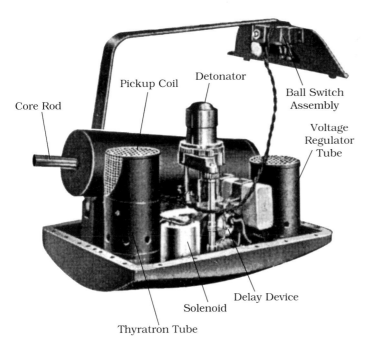

Core Rod

Pickup Coil

Detonator

Ball Switch Assembly

Voltage Regulator Tube

Thyratron Tube

Solenoid

Delay Device

The magnetic exploder (left) located in the warhead of the Mark 14 torpedo. The success of the submarine torpedo in World War I led the navies of the world to increase the armor plating along the sides of their larger warships. To counter this effort, U.S. torpedo designers in the early 1920s developed a magnetic exploder which could travel beneath a ship and detonate under its vulnerable keel. By 1926, the Navy's Bureau of Ordnance was ready to try the first exploders. Ideally, when the torpedo passed beneath a ship, the magnetic field from its steel hull would cause a firing pin to strike a primer cap and set off a detonator and the warhead's 643 pounds of TNT. The cost-conscious Bureau allowed just two live firings of the exploder, only one of which worked, before certifying the weapon. Failure to test the exploder mechanism masked magnetic sensitivity problems that prevented the exploder from working properly. U.S. submarines struggled with a defective torpedo for the first two years of the war.

China

Thailand

Indo-china

Camranh Bay

USS Sargo's First War Patrol
December 11–27, 1941

After the bombing of Cavite Naval Station, Captain John Wilkes, Acting Commander of U.S. Asiatic Submarines, deployed his boats to locate and intercept the expected invasion force. Three submarines—*Pickerel, Spearfish,* and *Sargo*—went to patrol off the Japanese naval base at Camranh Bay, Indochina. *Sargo,* commanded by Lt. Comdr. Tyrrell Jacobs, sighted its first vessel on December 14th. It fired a torpedo at the 4,000 ton cargo ship only

to have the weapon explode halfway to the target. Jacobs believed the Mark 6 magnetic exploder had malfunctioned and decided as a precaution to deactivate the device on the rest of his torpedoes. Ten days later he fired five torpedoes at two freighters and missed again. After another failed attack a few days later, the frustrated Jacobs guessed the torpedoes were also running too deep. He changed the depth settings and waited for another ship to test his theory. On January 4, 1942 *Sargo* spotted a slow-moving tanker. After a painstaking 35

minute approach, he fired one torpedo from 1,200 yards only to have it miss. Now fed up, Jacobs broke radio silence and sent a dispatch to Captain Wilkes describing the Mark 14's problems. The Navy Bureau of Ordnance rejected complaints about the torpedoes and blamed the submarine captains for the unsuccessful patrols. Nevertheless, the issues raised by Jacobs refused to go away. It took 18 months before the Navy finally solved the Mark 14's three design problems.

Invasion of the Dutch East Indies

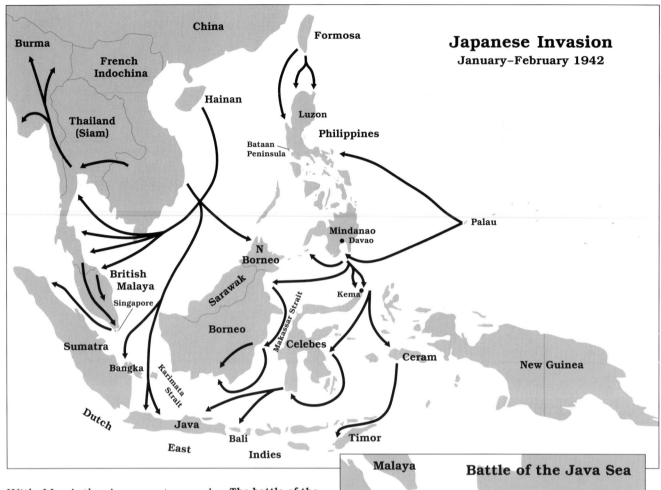

With MacArthur's army trapped in Bataan, the Japanese seized the southern Philippines and massed naval forces at Davao for the invasion of the Dutch East Indies. Admiral Thomas Hart ordered 11 U.S. submarines to blockade the port, but the Japanese fleet sailed before the submarines arrived.

The invasion force split into an eastern and western wing to attack the islands of Borneo and Celebes simultaneously. Captain John Wilkes managed to place seven submarines along the Makassar Strait to intercept the western fleet. They made several attacks, but sank no Japanese ships, and submarine S-36 was lost on a reef. Swordfish torpedoed the 4,000 ton freighter Myoken Maru in Kema harbor on January 24th. In the same area, on Feb-

The battle of the Java Sea (right) took place on February 27, 1942. Fourteen Allied warships attacked a Japanese invasion convoy. The Japanese won the battle, and cleared the way to land their forces on Java.

ruary 11th, Japanese destroyers sank the U.S. submarine Shark. By the end of January the Imperial Navy controlled Borneo and Celebes, and prepared to invade Java.

Captain Wilkes, expecting the next Japanese attack at Timor Island, shifted his 17 available submarines away from Java to ambush the invasion. However, the main attack was aimed at Java and almost 100 transports

escorted by 40 warships sailed safely through the unguarded Karimata and Makassar Straits. Once again U.S. subs came into the battle area late and made several unsuccessful attacks. On February 27th the Japanese destroyed the last surviving Allied cruiser force north of Australia in the Battle of the Java Sea. The Dutch surrendered the islands to the Japanese on March 12th.

Loss in Action Report:

"Perch attempted to engage the enemy with her three-inch deck gun but it could neither be trained nor elevated and the sights were shattered. Torpedoes could not be fired. In this helpless condition, with no fire power, obviously unable to submerge, and capable of making only five knots on the surface, the Commanding Officer decided to abandon and scuttle the boat at once. All hands were ordered topside. The diving alarm was sounded and the vents were opened by one officer who remained below for this purpose. The men on deck literally felt the ship, which was still going ahead at one-third speed on her batteries, go out from under them. All the men leaving the ship were equipped with life jackets, and some, in addition, carried escape lungs and flashlights. The officer who manned the vents had to fight his way out through the open conning tower hatch against the incoming water. Perch went down about 100 yards from the survivors shortly before dawn on 3 March 1942, with her colors flying."

Lt. Comdr. David A. Hurt (top) captain of the submarine *Perch.*

When the Japanese invasion of Java got underway in late February 1942, USS *Perch* was among the submarines assigned to a last-ditch defense of the island. Patrolling off Surabaya on the night of March 1st, *Perch* encountered Japanese destroyers, *Hatsukaze* and *Amatsukaze.* The warships closed in and depth-charged the submarine. Explosions damaged two engines and wrecked the periscopes. *Perch* stayed on the bottom for 16 hours then surfaced after sunset. The boat could not submerge again, and later that night the Japanese destroyers moved in for the kill. Captain Hurt scuttled his ship at dawn on March 3, 1942. The Japanese picked up the crew and sent them to Japan as POWs.

USS *Perch* (below) at sea before the war.

Depth Charge Attack on USS Perch

147 ft.

Withdrawal to Australia

The Allied naval disaster in the Java Sea on February 27, 1942 ended effective military resistance to the Japanese in the Dutch East Indies and forced the remaining Allied ships south to Australia. Captain John Wilkes, Acting Commander of U.S. Asiatic Submarines, had already ordered the sub tender *Holland* and five submarines to leave Java. The day after the battle he departed on the submarine *Spearfish*.

Holland arrived in Fremantle, on the southwestern coast of Australia, on March 3rd. Fortunately two U.S. supply ships waited in the harbor to replenish *Holland's* exhausted stores. Captain Wilkes wasted no time in setting up a new submarine base. He leased buildings along the Fremantle docks for machine shops and storage areas, then established his headquarters in nearby Perth. Wilkes ordered the dozen or so U.S. submarines still north of Java to finish their war patrols and proceed south to Fremantle.

Captain Wilkes was still organizing his command post when he received orders to send a submarine to the Philippines to evacuate General MacArthur and his family to Australia. *Permit* left its station off Java and sailed north, reaching the island of Corregidor on March 15, 1942. By the time the submarine arrived, MacArthur had already departed on a PT boat. Nevertheless, *Permit* evacuated 36 important codebreakers.

Two U.S. submarines extracted a small measure of revenge from the Japanese before reaching Australia. On March 2nd, Commander Richard Voge in *Sailfish* sank the 6,440 ton *Kamogawa Maru*, a large naval aircraft ferry, north of Bali. Two days later, James "Red" Coe in *S-39* sank the large fleet tanker, *Erimo*, in the Java Sea.

General Douglas MacArthur (above) in 1942. After leaving the Philippines with his famous "I shall return" promise, he established his headquarters in Australia and became Supreme Allied Commander of the Southwest Pacific area.

Fremantle, Australia (right). After the evacuation from Java, the U.S. Asiatic Submarine Force commander set up a base in Fremantle, the closest Allied port to the occupied Dutch East Indies. U.S. submarines based in Fremantle sank 340 Japanese ships during the Pacific war.

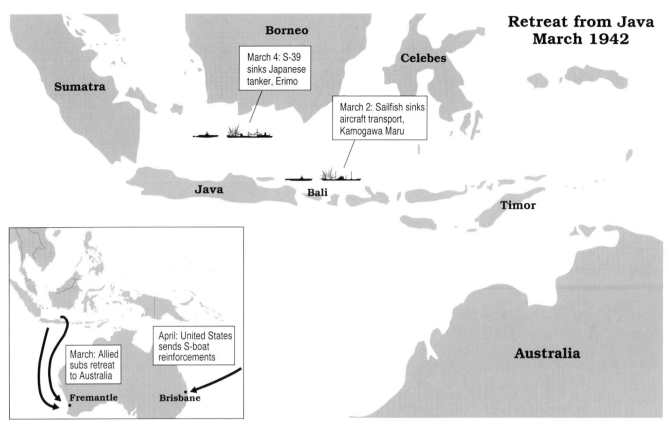

Retreat from Java
March 1942

Borneo

March 4: S-39 sinks Japanese tanker, Erimo

Celebes

Sumatra

March 2: Sailfish sinks aircraft transport, Kamogawa Maru

Java

Bali

Timor

March: Allied subs retreat to Australia

April: United States sends S-boat reinforcements

Fremantle

Brisbane

Australia

The Allied retreat to Australia (inset above) in March 1942 marked the low point for the U.S. Asiatic Submarine Force. In four months of war they had sunk only ten Japanese ships.

Brisbane, Australia (left). Eleven S-boats arrived in Brisbane in April 1942 to help protect Australia's eastern coast. Although not designed to operate in equatorial heat and humidity, the Submarine Command sent them on war patrols into the Solomon Islands, where they sank several Japanese ships, including the heavy cruiser *Kako*.

Destination Corregidor

The collapse of General Douglas MacArthur's fight-on-the-beach defense strategy in the Philippines forced 100,000 U.S. and Philippine troops into the Bataan Peninsula before proper provision could be made for food, ammunition, and medical supplies. Within a few weeks hunger and disease began to exact a greater toll from the Allies than the Japanese siege.

Lacking a fleet to overcome the Japanese blockade of Bataan and Corregidor, desperate American authorities in Australia turned to submarines to bring in small amounts of supplies and to evacuate key personnel. On Friday January 16th, *Seawolf* sailed from Darwin, Australia loaded with 675 boxes of .50 caliber ammunition. The submarine tied up at Corregidor's south dock on the night of January 27th and after unloading, took 25 pilots aboard for evacuation to Java.

A week later, on February 3rd, *Trout* arrived from Pearl Harbor with 3,500 three-inch shells. After leaving off the ammunition, *Trout's* captain, Frank Fenno, asked the naval commander at Corregidor for 25 tons of ballast. Naval authorities astonished Fenno by loading two tons of gold and 18 tons of silver, belonging to the Philippine government.

Five more submarines reached Corregidor in the next two months: *Seadragon, Swordfish, Permit, Spearfish,* and *Snapper. Spearfish* arrived just before the fortress fell on May 6, 1942. The submarine evacuated 12 officers, 12 Army nurses, the wife of a Navy officer, and a complete roster of U.S. personnel on Corregidor. A few hours after departing the island *Spearfish* received a last message from the embattled defenders: "One hundred and seventy-three officers and 2,317 men of the Navy reaffirm their loyalty and devotion to country, families, and friends."

Submarine Runs to Corregidor

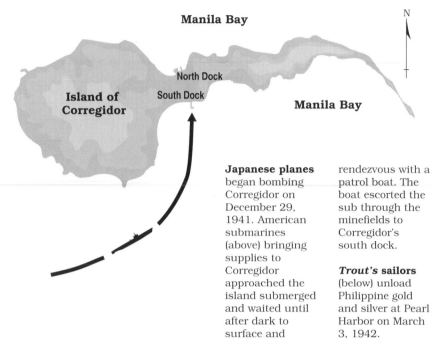

Manila Bay

North Dock
South Dock

Island of Corregidor

Manila Bay

N

Japanese planes began bombing Corregidor on December 29, 1941. American submarines (above) bringing supplies to Corregidor approached the island submerged and waited until after dark to surface and rendezvous with a patrol boat. The boat escorted the sub through the minefields to Corregidor's south dock.

***Trout's* sailors** (below) unload Philippine gold and silver at Pearl Harbor on March 3, 1942.

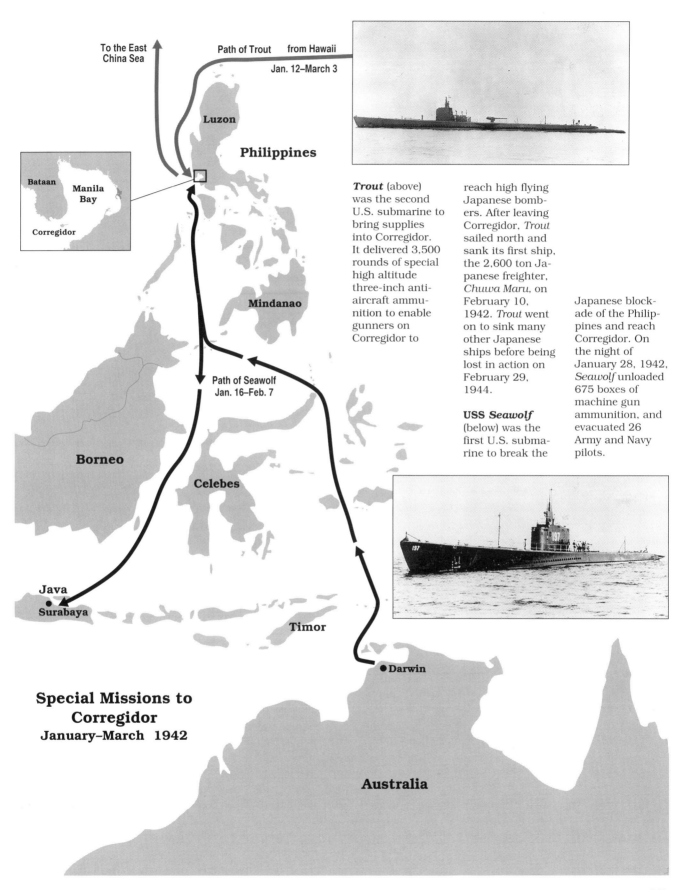

To the East
China Sea

Path of Trout   from Hawaii
Jan. 12–March 3

Luzon

Philippines

Bataan

Manila
Bay

Corregidor

Mindanao

Path of Seawolf
Jan. 16–Feb. 7

Borneo

Celebes

Java
●Surabaya

Timor

●Darwin

**Special Missions to
Corregidor**
January–March 1942

Australia

Trout (above) was the second U.S. submarine to bring supplies into Corregidor. It delivered 3,500 rounds of special high altitude three-inch anti-aircraft ammunition to enable gunners on Corregidor to reach high flying Japanese bombers. After leaving Corregidor, *Trout* sailed north and sank its first ship, the 2,600 ton Japanese freighter, *Chuwa Maru*, on February 10, 1942. *Trout* went on to sink many other Japanese ships before being lost in action on February 29, 1944.

USS *Seawolf* (below) was the first U.S. submarine to break the Japanese blockade of the Philippines and reach Corregidor. On the night of January 28, 1942, *Seawolf* unloaded 675 boxes of machine gun ammunition, and evacuated 26 Army and Navy pilots.

37

Unrestricted Submarine Warfare

Two days after the surrender of Corregidor, American carrier task forces turned back a Japanese amphibious invasion in the battle of the Coral Sea. Although the battle cost the U.S. aircraft carrier *Lexington*, it marked the first time a Japanese fleet had been stopped since the beginning of the war. A momentary calm settled on the Southwest Pacific. Admiral Yamamoto postponed further attacks aimed at Australia until he could destroy the U.S. Fleet at Midway in the central Pacific.

At the same time, the arrival of a new squadron of submarines at Pearl Harbor and the opening of U.S. sub bases in Fremantle and Brisbane allowed American commanders to mount 27 war patrols in May 1942.

In spite of continuing problems with the Mark 14 torpedo, U.S. submarines achieved some important successes. In the East China Sea, *Triton* sank a trawler, three freighters, and the Japanese submarine *I-64*. On May 8, 1942 *Grenadier* torpedoed the large 14,500 ton passenger vessel, *Taiyo Maru,* carrying hundreds of Japanese oil technicians and engineers to the Dutch East Indies to restore damaged oil fields. Captain James "Red" Coe, in *Skipjack,* sank three freighters in the South China Sea.

On its first patrol off the east coast of Japan, *Drum* sank the important seaplane carrier, *Mizuho,* and three cargo ships. Altogether, U.S. submarines sank 29 Japanese ships in May 1942—the highest monthly total to date in the war.

A merchant ship (above) torpedoed by USS *Drum.* In May 1942, 27 U.S. submarines patrolled the Pacific. Eighteen boats from Pearl Harbor covered the coast of Japan, the East China Sea, and the Marshall and Caroline islands. Five fleet submarines sailed from Fremantle and one, *Spearfish,* made the last run to Corregidor before the fortress fell. Four old S-class subs from Brisbane patrolled the Solomon Islands.

USS *Drum* at dock (above). Commissioned in late 1941, *Drum* sank seven Japanese ships in 1942, five in 1943, and three more in 1944. The submarine ended the war with 14 large merchant ships and the seaplane carrier, *Mizuho,* to its official credit.

Hokkaido

***Drum* left Pearl** Harbor on its first war patrol on April 17, 1942. At midnight two weeks later off Nagoya, Japan, *Drum* torpedoed a large ship. Unknown to *Drum's* captain, Lt. Comdr. Robert Rice, he had sunk the 9,000 ton seaplane carrier, *Mizuho.* The carrier had been an important part of the Philippines invasion force and was returning to Japan for refit. *Drum* went on to sink three merchantmen during its 31 day patrol.

Honshu

Shonan Maru
May 13

Kitakata Maru
May 25

Mizuho
May 2

Shikoku

Unknown Freighter
May 9

Kyushu

Japan, May 1942
Ships Sunk by USS Drum

Manning M. Kimmel was one of the officers aboard *Drum* on its first war patrol. He was the oldest son of Admiral Husband Kimmel who was commander

Manning M. Kimmel
USS *Drum*

of the Pacific Fleet on December 7, 1941. The U.S. government found the elder Kimmel partially responsible for the Pearl Harbor attack and forced him to resign from the Navy. Manning Kimmel and his brother Thomas, both in submarines, were eager to clear the family name by successful war records. After serving on *Drum* and *Raton* as executive officer, Kimmel achieved command of *Robalo* in the summer of 1944. While returning from a patrol off Indochina the *Robalo* hit a mine and sank.

A Vulnerable Empire

No major industrial country in the world was more dependent on its merchant marine than Japan. Without natural resources and adequate agricultural land, the Japanese imported one-third of the total raw materials used by industry and about 20 percent of the nation's food supply. Most of the feedstocks for the iron, steel, aluminum, and chemical industries—all basic to the manufacture of munitions—came from overseas. Even more critical, tankers brought in 82 percent of the petroleum needed to drive the Imperial Army and Navy.

At the outbreak of war, the Army and Navy requisitioned two-thirds of all available merchant ships to carry out military operations, causing an acute shortage of shipping for the civilian economy. Hundreds of borrowed vessels transported the Imperial Army's soldiers and equipment to Malaya, the Philippines and the Dutch East Indies. Japanese planners knew the remaining civilian tonnage could not sustain the home island's heavy industries, but they hoped a quick victory would allow most of the ships to return to nonmilitary use before production dropped. However, the length of the war and the increasing U.S. submarine attacks on merchant ships prevented this outcome.

After the war ended, in 1945, the United States Strategic Bombing Survey concluded the following: "The war against shipping was the most decisive single factor in the collapse of the Japanese economy and the logistic support for Japanese military and naval power. Submarines accounted for the majority of vessel sinkings."

A profile of a Japanese World War II merchant ship (below). U.S. submariners used ship recognition manuals (bottom) to identify enemy vessels. Thanks to its military-directed building programs in the 1930s, Japan had amassed a fleet of 1,500 steel cargo ships and 94 oil tankers by 1941. Total shipping peaked in April 1942 and thereafter declined from war losses.

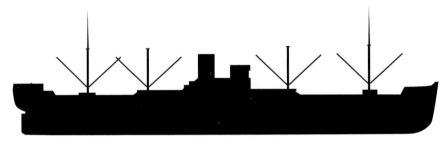

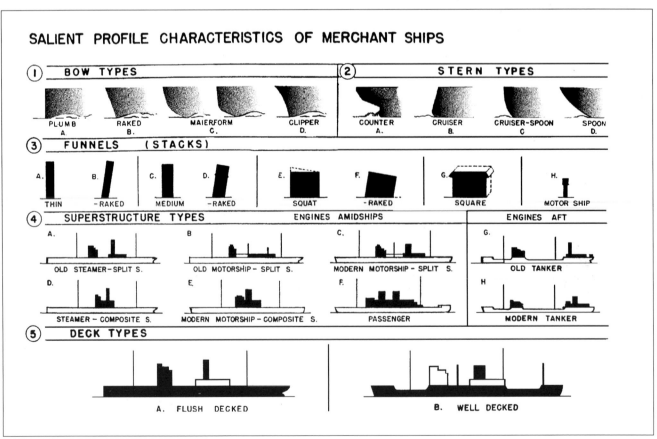

SALIENT PROFILE CHARACTERISTICS OF MERCHANT SHIPS

① BOW TYPES

PLUMB A.   RAKED B.   MAIERFORM C.   CLIPPER D.

② STERN TYPES

COUNTER A.   CRUISER B.   CRUISER-SPOON C.   SPOON D.

③ FUNNELS (STACKS)

A. THIN   B. –RAKED   C. MEDIUM   D. –RAKED   E. SQUAT   F. –RAKED   G. SQUARE   H. MOTOR SHIP

④ SUPERSTRUCTURE TYPES   ENGINES AMIDSHIPS   ENGINES AFT

A. OLD STEAMER–SPLIT S.   B. OLD MOTORSHIP–SPLIT S.   C. MODERN MOTORSHIP–SPLIT S.   G. OLD TANKER

D. STEAMER–COMPOSITE S.   E. MODERN MOTORSHIP–COMPOSITE S.   F. PASSENGER   H. MODERN TANKER

⑤ DECK TYPES

A. FLUSH DECKED   B. WELL DECKED

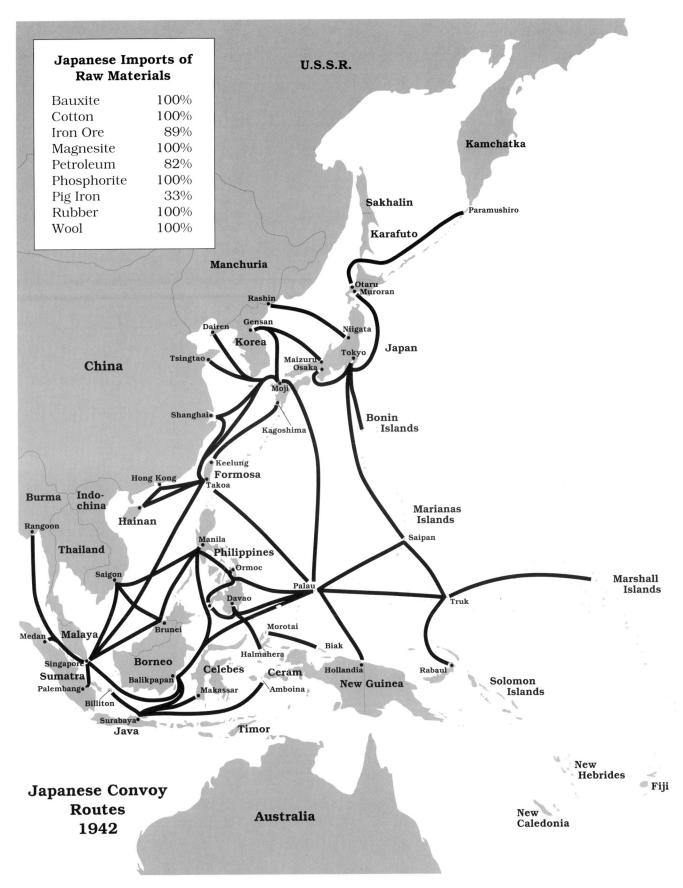

Japanese Imports of Raw Materials

Bauxite	100%
Cotton	100%
Iron Ore	89%
Magnesite	100%
Petroleum	82%
Phosphorite	100%
Pig Iron	33%
Rubber	100%
Wool	100%

U.S.S.R.

Kamchatka

Sakhalin

Karafuto

Paramushiro

Manchuria

Otaru
Muroran

Rashin

Dairen
Gensan
Niigata

Korea

Tsingtao

Maizuru
Osaka
Tokyo

Japan

China

Moji

Shanghai

Kagoshima

Bonin
Islands

Keelung

Hong Kong
Takoa

Formosa

Burma
Indo-
china

Hainan

Marianas
Islands

Saipan

Rangoon

Thailand

Manila

Philippines

Ormoc

Marshall
Islands

Saigon

Palau

Truk

Davao

Morotai

Brunei

Biak

Medan

Malaya

Halmahera

Singapore
Sumatra

Borneo
Balikpapan

Celebes

Ceram

Hollandia

New Guinea

Rabaul

Solomon
Islands

Palembang

Makassar

Amboina

Billiton

Surabaya
Java

Timor

New
Hebrides

Fiji

**Japanese Convoy
Routes
1942**

Australia

New
Caledonia

41

ULTRA—The Secret Weapon

In the first disastrous months of the Pacific War, radio intelligence (radio traffic analysis and cryptanalysis) gave the U.S. Navy invaluable information on Japanese tactical and strategic operations. A string of listening posts situated around the Pacific gathered encoded Japanese radio signals and transmitted them to three Navy codebreaking stations for analysis.

In 1939 the Japanese Foreign Ministry introduced a difficult machine-encoded cipher the U.S. Army Signal Intelligence Service called "Purple." In an 18-month effort, the Army's chief cryptanalyst, William Friedman, led a team that solved the cipher and reverse-engineered the Japanese coding machine (right). By 1940 they designated the intercepted Japanese messages "Magic," a term applied to all cryptographic intelligence until replaced by the British term "Ultrasecret" or "Ultra."

Laurance Frye Safford (above) founded the U.S. Navy's cryptanalytic office in 1924. His group set up the Pacific radio station intercept network and broke the first Japanese naval codes in the mid-1920s.

Commander Laurance F. Safford headed station Negat in Washington D.C. Commander Joseph J. Rochefort ran station Hypo at Pearl Harbor, and cryptanalysts evacuated by submarine from Corregidor in March 1942 manned station Belconnen in Melbourne, Australia.

While the codebreakers worked day and night to decipher the Imperial Navy's main operational code, JN25, other analysts used radio traffic to locate the call signs of Japanese fleet units, to ascertain which ships worked together, and to listen for increased radio volumes, indicating military operations. Using this intelligence, Admiral Nimitz launched a series of carrier air attacks on Japanese outposts around the Pacific. The most successful raid took place on March 18, 1942 when 104 U.S. aircraft heavily damaged an 18-ship invasion convoy off New Guinea. Although the Japanese occupied their targets of Lae and Salamaua, this bold attack forced them to postpone their planned assault on Port Morseby until early May. By that time, deciphered information provided by the codebreakers at Pearl Harbor allowed Nimitz to concentrate his carriers and repel the second Japanese invasion fleet at the Battle of the Coral Sea.

Meanwhile, Rochefort's Hypo cryptanalysis group at Pearl Harbor continued to make progress in deciphering JN25. On May 10th they discovered the outline for a Japanese offensive into the central Pacific, scheduled for early June. Admiral Yamamoto had decided to try to end the troubling carrier raids by drawing the U.S. Pacific Fleet into a decisive battle off Midway.

Rochefort and the JN25 Code

In June 1941 Joseph Rochefort (left), a 43-year-old career navy officer, took command of the codebreaking station Hypo at Pearl Harbor. A brilliant crypt-analyst, he spent two years in the 1920s working with Laurance Safford in the

Navy's crypto-graphic section. The service sent him to Japan in 1929 where he became fluent in Japanese. His critical work on JN25 in the spring of 1942 created the opportunity for the U.S. victory at Midway.

The Imperial Navy introduced JN25 as its main operational code in June 1939. It consisted of a dictionary of 33,333 naval terms each represented by a different five-digit numeral. The message was encoded by adding a key of other five-digit numbers. The Japanese changed to a new version of the code just before Pearl Harbor, but by March 1942 Rochefort's Hypo group could read enough of the new code to allow Admiral Nimitz to organize for the battles of the Coral Sea and Midway.

```
54975 66912 75783 28764 56985 61822 15791 42587
08758 70522 57818 39541 29874 24677 58951 35845
01721 76750 85274 67088 76823 72876 87087 63875
02679 72568 08764 25080 07143 49788 29136 47253
98215 78976 53521 58185 61494 87156 00618 72767
21379 88205 21555 74417 34194 28053 18050 61605
77200 30978 97256 21894 27407 56081 72762 84250
21379 82821 85588 72780 14329 28738 50756 18407
01637 95287 68165 23941 98351 65165 22971 97542
15465 46541 07841 099    5237 55821   72219 61237
03321 29752 85687 592
59554 72196 21794 75
75325 36754 45921 98
45463 58226 91872 97
83125 41215 79037 2
27647 90312 46798 2
92154 87349 66528 0
27618 91535 90323
90213 44662 65908
10058 84659 25542
73466 46552 88540
35872 46028 75672
52317 23189 65128
51252 88228 52458
54845 46650 5618
31530 57819 1087
81639 25737 5975
31154 84871 984
54879 75141 347
73750 20902 416
15976 37579 197
54279 61016 05
46942 15467 42
94164 29649 53
46319 08020 3
87978 52862 1
52059 21515 2
```

```
18191 46372 28201 15468 46072 54684 46504 40685
98904 54812 15465 48735 46465 46874 16766 69879
80461 65708 73789 79054 69544 74386 96339 65406
76454 61057 68743 89046 48796 87386 78376 97787
87637 40876 78699 76864 73541 35476 87414 63506
81321 35876 53546 10533 38735 14358 02534 68735
13045 24685 60465 22546 87651 36565 65453 16503
21158 79879 75978 56468 36765 46879 41387 51698
74053 12547 63658 38073 68796 80159 47635 95877
28598 46514 79847 27462 12176 85943 17378 59475
11631 09468 47965 38368 11796 48904 68756 94548
73102 61654 36546 54635 43216 85790 87354 98798
79206 38374 97208 57278 04023 18754 82871 67808
75491 24764 75275 25712 31648 13561 50614 78710
87675 49858 50705 64568 77897 27897 57912 14534
16546 48786 79535 94778 56758 05861 51402 87017
61060 41085 70658 25167 54857 80856 35575 70765
54787 85542 45857 55875 76087 00561 84854 37670
87564 17570 58701 15768 95876 59175 09854 78716
53615 88634 73568 95906 88657 60540 98456 54765
76404 56565 76848 10748 26525 58987 89727 49512
24757 59854 22278 79588 35475 25870 87087 60687
06870 68767 50586 58795 87454 57579 62007 45646
81218 75478 18797 47178 96849 76847 18217 02387
26465 70585 87694 75892 12838 87085 76745 57406
11758 74178 51581 29315 64325 68756 32782 01988
72876 92155 20875 08751 87567 80875 27807 55784
95287 32865 50817 57895 47587 18794 16549 68486
13270 74971 94154 95745 84170 76437 41574 58501
66357 74875 10856 54774 75952 58958 28932 82586
79694 89705 70751 87940 07197 42496 87501 81273
97086 51748 04518 87989 08917 76808 18751 51876
```

Midway

Warned by Rochefort's Pearl Harbor codebreakers in late May 1942 of Yamamoto's coming invasion, Admiral Nimitz prepared his forces to attack the Japanese Fleet. He reinforced Midway with ground troops and land-based aircraft, positioned his three American carriers northwest of the expected Japanese track to wait in ambush, and concentrated all available fleet submarines in the battle area.

Eleven submarines patrolled in a defensive arc around the small American outpost. Four more protected the area halfway between Pearl Harbor and Midway, while four subs waited 300 miles from Honolulu, Hawaii as a rear guard. *Cuttlefish* held a lonely spot 700 miles west of Midway.

The carrier air battle developed on the morning of June 4th to the northwest of the main arc of submarines and only *Nautilus* managed an attack on the enemy fleet. Although unsuccessful, this attack had a crucial effect on the battle. Shortly after *Nautilus* fired its torpedoes, the Japanese changed course northward to prepare their own assault on the U.S. carriers.

The Japanese left the destroyer *Arashi* behind to depth-charge *Nautilus*. Two hours later, 32 U.S. dive-bombers from the carrier *Enterprise*, running low on gasoline and unable to find the enemy, sighted *Arashi* racing north to catch up with the striking force and tailed it. At 10:20 a.m., the *Enterprise* squadron, led by Lt. Comdr. Wade McClusky, bombed and fatally damaged Japan's heavy carriers, *Akagi* and *Kaga*. *Yorktown* dive-bombers sank the aircraft carrier *Soryu* at the same time. The next day U.S. planes destroyed the last Japanese carrier, *Hiryu*. Accepting defeat, Admiral Yamamoto ordered the invasion force to return to Japan.

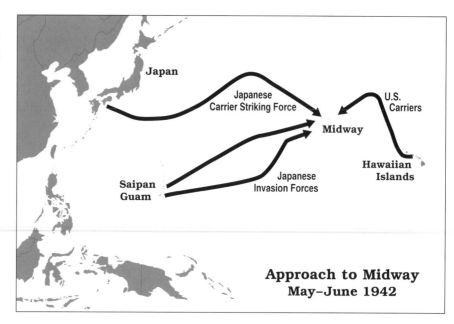

**Approach to Midway
May–June 1942**

Nautilus **followed** the Japanese carrier force northward and at noon spotted several columns of smoke on the horizon. The nearest one proved to be the burning Japanese carrier, *Kaga*, damaged in the 10:20 a.m. U.S. dive-bomber attack. Captain William Brockman brought *Nautilus* to 2,700 yards and fired three torpedoes. Two missed and the third failed to explode.

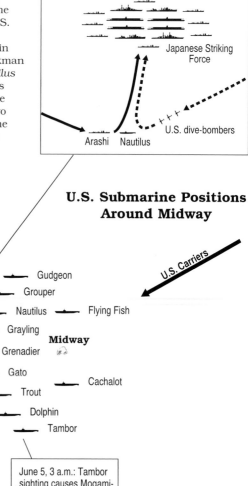

U.S. Submarine Positions Around Midway

June 4, 8:30 a.m.: Nautilus attacks Striking Force unsuccessfully. Force turns north, leaving destroyer, Arashi, to depth-charge Nautilus.

Japanese Carrier Striking Force

U.S. Carriers

Gudgeon
Grouper
Nautilus — Flying Fish
Grayling
Midway
Grenadier
Gato
Cachalot
Trout
Dolphin
Tambor

Japanese Invasion Forces

June 5, 3 a.m.: Tambor sighting causes Mogami-Mikuma collision

Mogami-Mikuma Collision

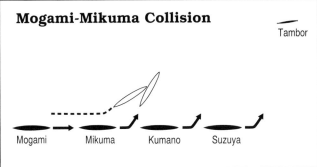

Tambor

Mogami   Mikuma   Kumano   Suzuya

After the loss of his carriers, Admiral Yamamoto made a last-ditch attempt to salvage the battle by sending four fast heavy cruisers to bombard Midway. Shortly before 3 a.m. they sighted the U.S. submarine *Tambor.* The cruiser task force commander ordered an emergency turn but *Mogami* did not receive the message and collided with its sister ship, *Mikuma.* The collision damaged both ships and reduced their speed to 17 knots. For the next two days U.S. aircraft bombed the two cruisers, sinking *Mikuma* and wrecking *Mogami* (top). Although *Nautilus* and *Tambor* sank no ships directly, both submarines made important contributions to the U.S. victory at Midway.

Midway Atoll (right). The battle of Midway in June 1942 turned the tide of the war.

War in the Aleutians

The Japanese bombed Dutch Harbor in the eastern Aleutians on June 3, 1942 as a diversionary feint to their doomed attack on Midway. Three days later they invaded Attu and Kiska in the western Aleutians with an eye toward preventing an Allied move against Japan's Kurile Islands. The U.S. Navy had six S-boats based at Dutch Harbor in May 1942, but they proved difficult to operate in the frozen, storm-lashed waters of the Aleutians. Admiral Nimitz decided to reinforce the S-boats with eight modern fleet submarines after the Battle of Midway.

The fleet boats went into action immediately. *Triton*, patrolling off Agattu Island, torpedoed and sank the 1,600 ton destroyer *Nenohi* on July 4, 1942. The next day, 150 miles to the east off Kiska Island, *Growler* spotted three Japanese destroyers anchored in a line outside the main harbor. *Growler*, commanded by Howard Gilmore, a well-liked skipper, quietly approached the destroyers at slow speed and fired three Mark 14 torpedoes. All hit their targets. The destroyer *Arare* sank, and *Kasumi* and *Shiranuhi* suffered heavy damage.

Ten days later, on July 15th, *Grunion,* on its first war patrol, torpedoed and sank two submarine chasers. *Grunion* continued to operate in the heavily-patrolled Kiska area but failed to return after a last message to Dutch Harbor on July 30th—probably the victim of an unrecorded depth charge attack.

The Japanese remained in possession of Attu until May 1943 and Kiska until July 1943. The islands proved to be a strategic drain on the Japanese and the savage weather was the most consistent enemy for both navies.

Triton in the Aleutians (left) in July 1942 after its successful 4th war patrol.

Grunion (below) vanished off Kiska while on its first patrol in early August 1942.

Attu

Agattu

July 4: Triton sinks Japanese destroyer, Nenoni

Early August: Grunion is lost; possibly depth-charged

July 5: Growler sinks destroyer, Arare, and damages two others, Kasumi and Shiranui

Kiska

ALASKA

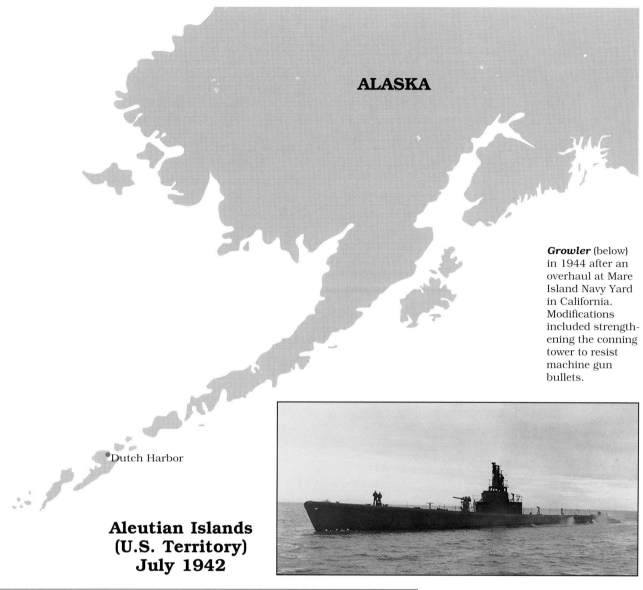

Dutch Harbor

Growler (below) in 1944 after an overhaul at Mare Island Navy Yard in California. Modifications included strengthening the conning tower to resist machine gun bullets.

Aleutian Islands (U.S. Territory) July 1942

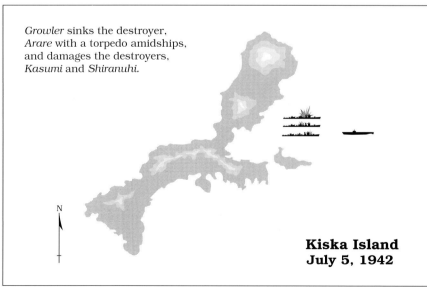

Growler sinks the destroyer, *Arare* with a torpedo amidships, and damages the destroyers, *Kasumi* and *Shiranuhi.*

N

Kiska Island
July 5, 1942

When Growler put three Japanese destroyers out of commission in July 1942, it marked the beginning of an illustrious but tragic career. On its next war patrol in the East China Sea the submarine sank four merchant ships. Following this voyage, *Growler* transferred to Brisbane. On a rainy night during its fourth war patrol the submarine rammed a small Japanese supply ship and Captain Howard Gilmore was killed in the ensuing surface battle. He received a Medal of Honor for ordering his boat to submerge without him. *Growler* went on to complete ten war patrols and to sink ten enemy ships before it was lost with all hands during a convoy attack in the South China Sea on November 11, 1944.

Guadalcanal

After the victory at Midway, U.S. attention shifted to the South Pacific where Japanese forces on Guadalcanal in the Southern Solomons were building an airstrip. If completed, their planes could dominate northern Australia. Utilizing the U.S. 1st Marine Division, the Allies invaded Guadalcanal on August 7, 1942.

The Allies achieved surprise, but the Japanese counterattack was swift and deadly. Admiral Mikawa, Japanese commander at Rabaul, put together a scratch force of seven cruisers and a destroyer and headed for Guadalcanal.

U.S. sub *S-38* spotted the Japanese column and sent a warning to Australia, but the message was lost in the confusion. The next night off Savo Island the Japanese surprised the Allied naval force and sank four heavy cruisers.

On their return, the Japanese ran into U.S. submarine *S-44*, a few miles off their base at Kavieng, New Ireland. At 9 a.m. *S-44* torpedoed and sank the 8,800 ton heavy cruiser *Kako*, the first major Japanese warship sunk by a U.S. submarine in the war.

S-44's crew
(top) in August 1942. Captain Hank Munson watches from the bridge, while his sailors paint a rising sun flag on the conning tower after sinking the Japanese heavy cruiser *Kako* off New Ireland.

Submarine S-44
(right) at sea. This S-boat sank three Japanese ships, a record for its class, but was itself sunk by a Japanese destroyer on October 7, 1943 in the northern Kurile Islands.

48

Torpedoes hit the *Kako* (right) on the morning of August 10, 1942. Built in 1926 and modernized in 1937, the 8,100 ton heavy cruiser mounted six eight-inch guns and twelve 24-inch Long Lance torpedo tubes. *Kako* carried a crew of 625 men and could reach a speed of 34 knots. As part of Cruiser Division 6, it took part in the invasions of Guam, Wake, Rabaul, and the Coral Sea. At the Battle of Savo Island, *Kako* torpedoed and damaged the heavy cruiser, *Chicago* and helped sink U.S. cruisers, *Quincy*, *Astoria*, and *Vincennes*.

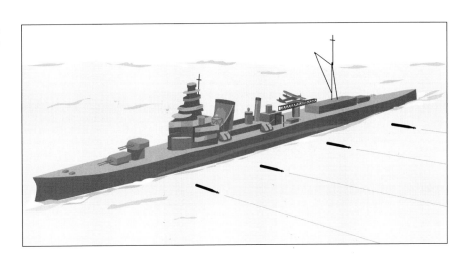

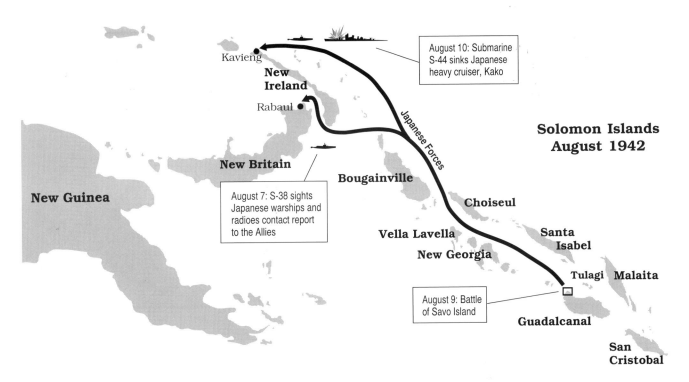

August 10: Submarine S-44 sinks Japanese heavy cruiser, Kako

Kavieng

New Ireland

Rabaul

New Britain

August 7: S-38 sights Japanese warships and radioes contact report to the Allies

New Guinea

Japanese Forces

Bougainville

Choiseul

Vella Lavella

New Georgia

Santa Isabel

Tulagi   Malaita

August 9: Battle of Savo Island

Guadalcanal

San Cristobal

Solomon Islands August 1942

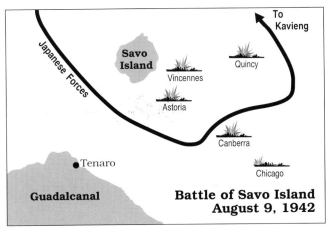

To Kavieng

Japanese Forces

Savo Island

Quincy

Vincennes

Astoria

Canberra

Chicago

Tenaro

Guadalcanal

Battle of Savo Island August 9, 1942

Admiral Mikawa's battle force of seven cruisers and a destroyer neared Guadalcanal at 1 a.m. on the moonless, overcast night of August 8–9th. It had evaded Allied air search planes and slipped past two patrolling U.S. destroyers which guarded approaches to the landing beaches.

At 1:38 a.m. the Japanese opened fire on the Australian cruiser, *Canberra* and the U.S. cruiser, *Chicago*. *Canberra* took 24 shell hits, and a Long Lance torpedo blew off *Chicago's* bow. The Japanese column swung north and 15 minutes later shelled and torpedoed U.S. cruisers, *Astoria*, *Vincennes*, and *Quincy*. By 2:30 a.m. it was all over. The Japanese retired at high speed, leaving four Allied cruisers sinking and one heavily damaged.

49

Makin Raid

In the summer of 1942 Admiral Nimitz planned a hit-and-run attack on Makin Island in the Gilbert Islands to gather intelligence and provide a diversion to the invasion of Guadalcanal. On August 8th, 221 marines of the 2nd Raider Battalion, led by Lt. Col. Evans Carlson, crammed into the Navy's two largest submarines, *Nautilus* and *Argonaut*, and sailed for Makin Island. Nine days later on August 17th at 2:30 a.m., the marines struggled ashore in 18 rubber boats, fighting strong winds and surf. They fanned out over the island and attacked the Japanese garrison of 44 men. *Nautilus* assisted the marines at 7 a.m. by firing 24 shells into a Japanese strong point, and then used its six-inch guns to sink a freighter and a patrol boat in the inner lagoon.

The marines killed most of the garrison but in the afternoon a dozen planes, including two large flying boats, strafed and bombed the American positions and brought Japanese reinforcements. At 6:30 p.m. Lt. Col. Carlson gave the order to return to the beach. High surf prevented the marines' evacuation to the submarines until the next night. The stunned Japanese did not interfere. Nine marines failed to reach the beach and were captured by the Japanese. They were taken to Kwajalein in the Marshall Islands and on October 16, 1942 executed as spies.

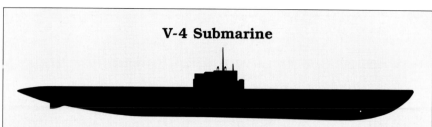

V-4 Submarine

Argonaut **(V-4)**, *Narwhal* (V-5), and *Nautilus* (V-6) were large 2,700 ton experimental submarines built in the late 1920s as part of the U.S. Navy's effort to design a fleet submarine. They turned out to be expensive, slow, hard to dive, and unmaneuverable. Nevertheless, all three boats served in World War II and compiled remarkable records. During the war, *Nautilus* sank six ships and *Narwhal* destroyed seven. In January 1943, *Argonaut* was lost with all hands during a destroyer counterattack. The submarines' great size allowed the Navy to use them for covert special missions. *Nautilus* and *Narwhal* transported 100 army scouts to the invasion of Attu in May 1943, and *Nautilus* returned to the Gilberts in November 1943 to land a marine detachment on the island of Abemama. Thereafter the two submarines became the backbone of a regular shuttle service, supplying the guerrilla movement in the Philippines. Between them they delivered hundreds of tons of ammunition, food, and medicines, landed many secret agents, and evacuated dozens of trapped civilians.

Makin is a triangular-shaped atoll two thousand miles southwest of Oahu. The main land forms are two islands, Butaritari and Kuma, which are thirteen miles long, but only an average 500 yards wide. The highest point on the islands is just 12 feet above sea level. The Japanese occupied Butaritari Island on December 10, 1941 and constructed a small seaplane base. After the U.S. Marine raid, the Japanese substantially reinforced Makin and Tarawa, their other stronghold in the Gilbert Islands.

Kuma Island

Butaritari Island

Pacific Ocean

□ Makin

Gilbert Islands

Japanese Fortification

Japanese Fortification

2:30 a.m.: Nautilus and Argonaut land Marines on the southern shore

Makin Atoll
August 17, 1942

Lt. Col. Evans Carlson, Capt. James Roosevelt, and J.R. Pierce, commander of the *Argonaut* (left). While serving with the Marines in Shanghai in the late 1930s, the charismatic Evans Carlson studied guerrilla tactics used by the Chinese Communists against the Japanese. He decided to adapt their methods, and beginning in January 1942 he turned the 2nd Raider Battalion into a tough commando unit trained to conduct special missions.

Nautilus and *Argonaut* (below), arriving back at Pearl Harbor with Carlson's exhausted raiders, are greeted by Admiral Nimitz and a brass band. The Makin raid cost the Marines 25 killed, 14 wounded, and 12 missing. After a short rest, Lt. Col. Carlson's battalion joined the 1st Marine Division in the Solomons on Guadalcanal. In late October they chased and partially destroyed a retreating Japanese regiment in a month-long battle in the jungle.

51

The Emperor's Front Door

The day the Marines evacuated Makin Island, a new submarine, *Guardfish*, arrived off northeast Honshu on its first Empire patrol. The U.S. Navy termed missions blockading Japan's coastal waters "Empire patrols."

Lt. Comdr. Thomas B. Klakring found thick merchant marine traffic along the east coast of Japan. After missing an 8,000 ton naval auxiliary on August 19th due to defective torpedoes, *Guardfish* boldly sank the 3,100 ton freighter *Seikai Maru* as it left Kinkasan Harbor on the afternoon of August 24th.

The next day, three more defective torpedoes denied the submarine its second freighter, and *Guardfish* headed north through heavy seas to the waters off Hokkaido. There, on September 2nd the sub torpedoed and sank the 2,300 ton freighter, *Teikyu Maru*, before turning south for another sweep.

Klarking decided to take *Guardfish* very close to shore and attack the coastal traffic from the unexpected land side. On the night of September 3rd the submarine charged its batteries and at dawn began working its way inshore. Tucked into the lee of Benton Bana point at 5:45 p.m. the next day, *Guardfish* ambushed and sank *Tenyu Maru* and *Kaimei Maru*. Two approaching freighters witnessed the carnage and fled into a nearby harbor. Klakring carefully maneuvered around the point to approach the mouth of the anchorage. In an extraordinary shot he fired a torpedo which traveled over four miles into the harbor and sank the 2,300 ton freighter, *Chita Maru*, which was riding at anchor alongside a large power plant and gas storage tank.

The next month the enraged Japanese planted an extensive mine field in the area to destroy future U.S. submarine raiders.

Periscope photos of three freighters sunk by *Guardfish* (left). In 1943 U.S. submarines began conducting periscope photographic reconnaissance of Japanese-held islands. *Nautilus'* survey of Tarawa's beaches prior to the attack on the Gilbert Islands corrected inaccurate charts. For the rest of the war U.S. submarines surveyed the beaches of each new invasion target.

Hokkaido

Teikyu Maru
Sept. 2

Tenyu Maru
Kaimei Maru
Chita Maru
Sept. 4

Seikai Maru
Aug. 24

Japan

Honshu

Shikoku

Kyushu

**Guardfish's First War Patrol
August–September 1942**

The crew of *Guardfish* (above) lined up for review. After awarding Lt. Comdr. Klakring the Navy Cross, the Submarine Command allowed *Life* magazine to run a story on *Guardfish's* first patrol, a rare wartime look at the security conscious "Silent Service." *Guardfish* spent two weeks at Midway for refit before setting out on its second patrol—this time to the East China Sea. On October 19th, *Guardfish* damaged a large freighter but was driven off by an alert patrol aircraft. Forty-eight hours later the submarine attacked and sank two large freighters in a convoy and once again evaded enemy planes. Bad weather closed in and *Guardfish* returned home, arriving at Pearl Harbor on November 28, 1942. The sub received a Presidential Unit Citation for these two outstanding patrols.

Minelaying

Throughout the war, U.S. submarines laid mines in a campaign of attrition against the coastal shipping routes and major ports of Japan and occupied East Asia. Ironically, a shortage of torpedoes during the Solomon's campaign forced submarines to start using the mines, which could also be launched from their 21-inch torpedo tubes.

Trigger sailed from Midway on December 7, 1942 with orders to lay two mine fields in the coastal waters of Japan just north of Tokyo Bay and then attack shipping. After careful reconnaissance, *Trigger* submerged on the moonlit night of December 20th and in 25 minutes laid a mine field just off Inubo Saki lighthouse. The approach of a large freighter interrupted the ejection of the second field and *Trigger* withdrew. The 8,500 ton cargo ship steamed into the mine field and blew up, the first victim of the newly planted Mark 12 magnetic mines.

Two days later, near one of the headlands which formed the entrance to Tokyo Bay, *Trigger* torpedoed *Teifuku Maru*, a 5,000 ton freighter. After these successes *Trigger's* crew spent Christmas Eve night off Tokyo Bay listening to holiday records over the P.A. system and thinking about their families thousands of miles away. Routine operations continued for the next two weeks until January 10th when *Trigger* spotted the destroyer, *Okikaze*, zig-zagging. The submarine struck the destroyer with two torpedoes and watched it sink on an even keel.

In addition to directly sinking enemy vessels, the minelaying campaign forced shipping away from protected coastal waters and into areas more vulnerable to sub attack. By war's end U.S. submarines had planted over 600 mines which sank at least 57 ships along Japanese shipping lanes.

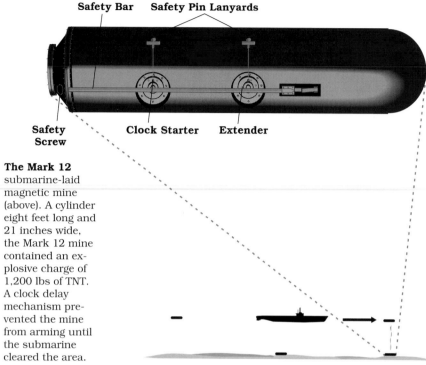

Mark 12 Mine

The Mark 12 submarine-laid magnetic mine (above). A cylinder eight feet long and 21 inches wide, the Mark 12 mine contained an explosive charge of 1,200 lbs of TNT. A clock delay mechanism prevented the mine from arming until the submarine cleared the area.

Submarine Minelaying Sept–Dec 1942

● = mine fields laid by U.S. submarines

In the fall of 1942 Pearl Harbor-based submarines, *Whale, Sunfish, Drum,* and *Trigger* planted four mine fields along the Japanese coast. Perth-based submarines, *Thresher, Gar, Grenadier, Tautog,* and *Tambor* planted five mine fields along Indochina.

Hokkaido

Mt. Fuji (above) as seen through *Trigger's* periscope. *Trigger* completed 11 war patrols, officially sank 18 ships, and received the Presidential Unit Citation. It sailed on its 12th patrol in early 1945 and was lost with all hands during an attack on a convoy on March 28, 1945 off Okinawa.

Honshu

Mt. Fuji

Dec. 20: Trigger lays two fields of Mark 12 mines in Japanese shipping lanes

From Pearl Harbor

To Midway

Jan. 10: Trigger sinks destroyer, Okikaze

Dec. 22: Trigger sinks Japanese freighter, Teifuku Maru

Shikoku

Kyushu

The Japanese destroyer, *Okikaze*, sinking (right). *Okikaze* belonged to the Minekaze class of destroyers. These 1,500 ton warships carried four 4.7-inch guns, two machine guns, and 36 depth charges. U.S. submarines sank eight of the 15 ships in this class.

Silversides

On December 17, 1942 USS *Silversides* left Brisbane on its fourth war patrol to the Bismarck Islands and Truk. Only five days later, off Japanese-held Bougainville, crewman George Platter developed acute appendicitis. Lt. Comdr. Creed Burlingame submerged the boat at 9:52 p.m. to allow his pharmacist's mate "a steadier platform" for removing the seaman's appendix.

Silversides surfaced after the operation and encountered a Japanese destroyer. Three hours and several depth charge attacks later, the submarine escaped the warship only to be assaulted by a patrol plane at 9 a.m. The aircraft's three bombs smashed the lights in the conning tower, threw men off their feet in the forward torpedo room, and jammed the bow planes. *Silversides* effected

The crew of *Silversides* fire the deck gun (above). On May 10, 1942 *Silversides* used its gun to shell a large sampan, and lost a gunner to enemy fire, the first American to die in a U.S. submarine gun attack.

Captain Creed C. Burlingame (inset above) was considered one of the more colorful commanders in the submarine service.

repairs that night and proceeded to its patrol station off Truk, Japan's main naval base in the south Pacific.

Two weeks later, on the night of January 18th, *Silversides* torpedoed and sank the 10,000 ton tanker, *Toei Maru.* In the ensuing depth charge attack the sub developed an oil leak. The leak caused an engine room fire and *Silversides* spent the next day struggling back into fighting trim.

Burlingame spotted a convoy on the night of January 20th and fired six torpedoes at the Japanese ships. Five torpedoes exploded and three freighters sank. The sixth torpedo of the salvo jammed halfway out the tube. The next morning Burlingame managed to fire the torpedo while backing at full speed. To add to his troubles, *Silversides* had an air leak, the No. 1 generator exploded once the sub moved forward, and a cereal box had lodged in the induction system. He wrote in his log: "Thus with a dangling torpedo with war head attached, a fuel and air leak, an explosion in a main generator, and Cream of Wheat in the main induction, all within two hours time, it was decided to leave the area two days ahead of schedule."

In December 1942, after five months of battles on Guadalcanal with the Americans, Imperial General Headquarters decided to abandon the island and set up a new defense line in the northern Solomons. Tokyo sent four convoys from Truk in January to deliver supplies to Rabaul. Utilizing Ultra information on January 20th, *Silversides* intercepted one of these convoys, consisting of four large freighters and two escorts. With five torpedoes *Silversides* sank three of the cargo ships.

Silversides **went** to the Navy Yard for overhaul after its tumultuous fourth patrol. Repairs completed, the submarine left Pearl Harbor in May 1943 and headed for the southwest Pacific. In Brisbane, John S. Coye relieved Burlingame as captain. He matched Burlingame's exploits on the seventh patrol when *Silversides* intercepted two convoys north of Rabaul and sank four merchantmen. *Silversides* sank three more ships in its next patrol off the Palaus and barely avoided three torpedoes fired by a Japanese submarine. In May 1944 *Silversides* sank six ships off the Marianas. *Silversides* finished 14 war patrols and received official credit for 23 Japanese ships sunk.

Pharmacist's Mate Thomas Moore performed an emergency appendectomy (below) aboard *Silversides* on December 22, 1942. The operation required four hours to complete. The patient, Fireman 3rd class George Platter, recovered and was standing watch six days later. Altogether, pharamacist's mates treated 11 cases of acute appendicitis without fatalities on U.S. submarines during World War II.

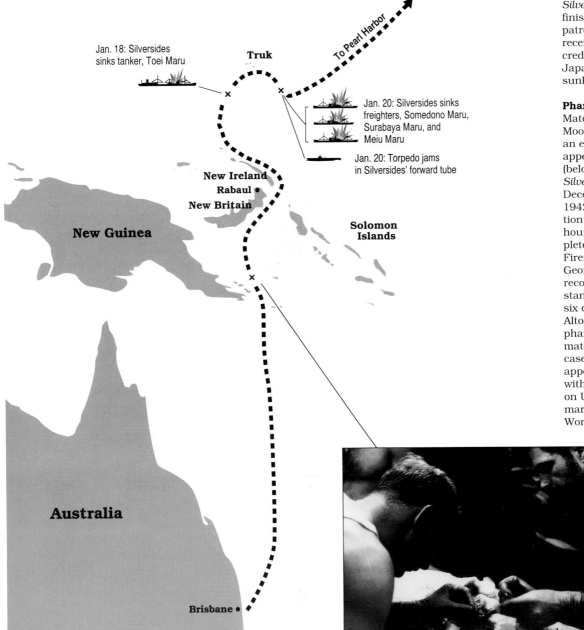

Jan. 18: Silversides sinks tanker, Toei Maru

Truk

To Pearl Harbor

Jan. 20: Silversides sinks freighters, Somedono Maru, Surabaya Maru, and Meiu Maru

Jan. 20: Torpedo jams in Silversides' forward tube

New Ireland
Rabaul ●
New Britain

New Guinea

Solomon Islands

Australia

Brisbane ●

January 1943

Thirteen months of war and 350 war patrols revealed the weaknesses and strengths of the U.S. submarine service. On the debit side, military necessity in the early months of the fighting diverted many submarines from commerce raiding into special missions: supplying Corregidor, evacuating personnel, landing commandos, and reconnaissance of the unmapped Japanese mandate islands. Pre-war military doctrine overemphasized the dangers of air attack, stressed extreme caution, and completely ignored the offensive potential of night surface attacks. This last mistake was particularly ironic because Hilter's U-boats demonstrated the tactical value of fighting on the surface off America's east coast throughout 1942. U.S. torpedoes often failed, although their tendency to run deep had been corrected. Eight U.S. submarines had been lost to enemy action.

On the credit side, the submarine force had grown from 51 boats on December 7, 1941 to 80 submarines on January 1, 1943. A strong, capable, and well-liked new admiral, Charles Lockwood, assumed command of Pearl Harbor-based subs. Approximately 180 Japanese ships—over 700,000 tons—had been sunk. These losses did not significantly reduce the quantity of raw materials flowing into Japan, but they prevented the growth of Japanese merchant shipping. The Imperial Navy failed to adopt a convoy system because the command resisted any defensive strategy at sea. As a consequence, American submarines did not suffer the terrible casualties German submarines experienced in the Atlantic in 1943.

It would be another year before increased shipping losses forced the Japanese to face the U.S. submarine menace.

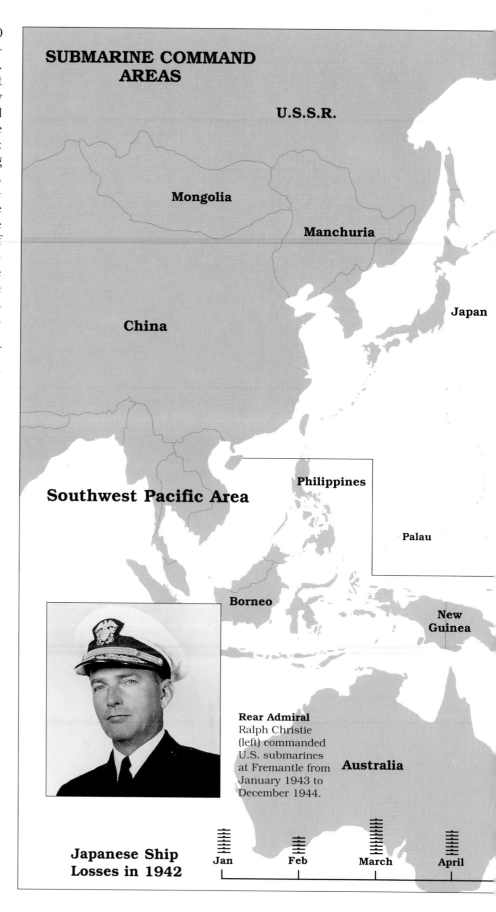

SUBMARINE COMMAND AREAS

U.S.S.R.

Mongolia

Manchuria

Japan

China

Philippines

Southwest Pacific Area

Palau

Borneo

New Guinea

Rear Admiral Ralph Christie (left) commanded U.S. submarines at Fremantle from January 1943 to December 1944.

Australia

Japanese Ship Losses in 1942

Jan Feb March April

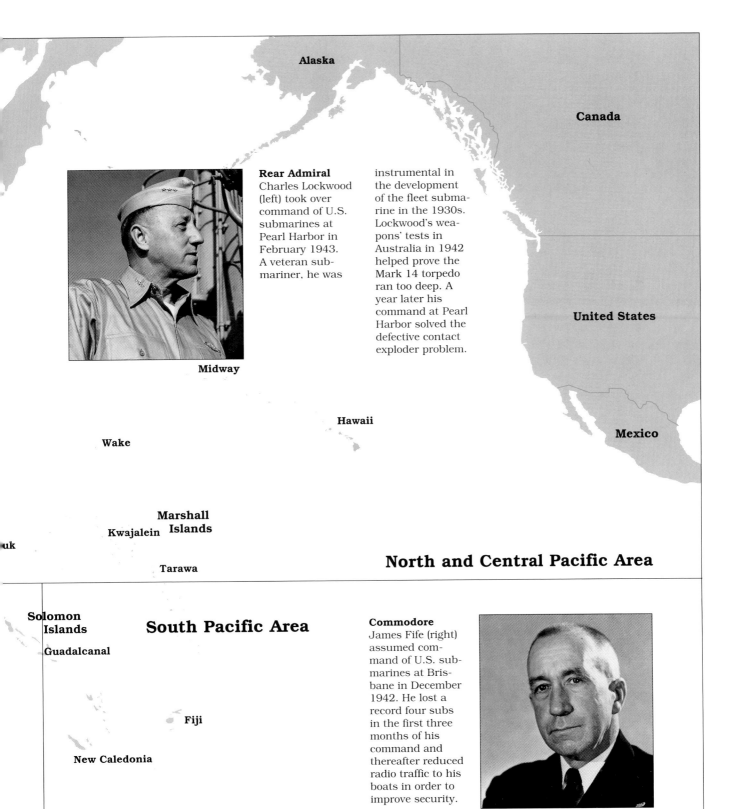

Alaska

Canada

Rear Admiral Charles Lockwood (left) took over command of U.S. submarines at Pearl Harbor in February 1943. A veteran submariner, he was instrumental in the development of the fleet submarine in the 1930s. Lockwood's weapons' tests in Australia in 1942 helped prove the Mark 14 torpedo ran too deep. A year later his command at Pearl Harbor solved the defective contact exploder problem.

United States

Midway

Hawaii

Wake

Mexico

Marshall Islands

Kwajalein

uk

Tarawa

North and Central Pacific Area

Solomon Islands

South Pacific Area

Guadalcanal

Commodore James Fife (right) assumed command of U.S. submarines at Brisbane in December 1942. He lost a record four subs in the first three months of his command and thereafter reduced radio traffic to his boats in order to improve security.

Fiji

New Caledonia

May	June	July	Aug	Sept	Oct	Nov	Dec

Reinforcements

The unexpected fall of France in June 1940 shocked the U.S. into a rapid expansion of the Navy. Along with many surface ships, Congress ordered 71 submarines commissioned in 1942–43. The new contracts were divided between the government-owned Portsmouth and Mare Island Navy Yards, and the privately-held Electric Boat Company, and Manitowoc Shipbuilding Company.

Portsmouth Navy Yard became famous for using prefabricated hull assemblies to produce submarines in record time. In 1944 Portsmouth built a submarine from keel to commissioning in an astounding 173 days and finished 81 submarines by the end of the war. Mare Island's smaller work force constructed 18 submarines before VJ day. The Electric Boat Company in Groton, Connecticut employed 12,000 men and women in its submarine yard and built 84 submarines by August 1945.

USS *Puffer* (above) launched on November 22, 1942. It was the fourth submarine the Manitowoc Shipbuilding Co. produced.

USS *Grouper's* hull (right) under construction at the Electric Boat Company in January 1941.

One submarine is finished (opposite) while another begins construction at the Electric Boat Yard.

The Bureau of Ships chose the Manitowoc Shipbuilding Company as a new submarine shipyard before the Pearl Harbor attack. Situated on a narrow river off Lake Michigan, Manitowoc launched its submarines sideways. After commissioning, the boats were towed down the Mississippi River in a floating dry dock. The innovative and hard working shipwrights of Manitowoc produced 28 submarines during the war. Thanks to these production miracles, 37 fleet submarines joined the Pacific campaign in 1942.

New Submarines Commissioned in 1942

January
Finback
Greenling
Trigger

February
Grouper

March
Growler
Haddock

April
Grunion
Halibut

May
Guardfish
Herring
Kingfish
Wahoo

June
Albacore
Amberjack
Shad
Whale

July
Barb
Blackfish
Runner
Sunfish

August
Gunnel
Sawfish

September
Gurnard
Scamp
Tunny

October
Haddo
Hake
Scorpion
Snook

November
Peto

December
Harder
Hoe
Steelhead

Take Her Down

On January 1, 1943 *Growler* departed Brisbane, Australia on its fourth war patrol. The submarine was commanded by Howard Gilmore, a fearless officer, well-liked by his crew, whose concern for his men included the habit of counting the watch to make sure no one was left behind when the submarine dived. Lt. Comdr. Gilmore took *Growler* to the Bismarck Sea to intercept the Japa-

Growler–Hayasaki Collision

nese reinforcements pouring into Rabaul. Defeat at Guadalcanal had only strengthened Japan's determination to hold onto the northern Solomons.

Finding the waters off Rabaul crowded with enemy ships, Gilmore torpedoed and sank the 5,800 ton passenger-cargo ship, *Chifuku Maru,* on January 16th and damaged another freighter on January 30th.

Brisbane ordered *Growler* west to a new area on the night of February 6th. Three hours after receiving the message, while proceeding on the surface at 17 knots, *Growler's* radar detected the 900 ton Japanese supply ship, *Hayasaki,* at 8,000 yards. The submarine closed this distance in

darkness broken by intermittent rain squalls which blacked out the radar. At 2,000 yards *Hayasaki* reversed course and the distance between the two ships rapidly decreased. Perhaps unsure of his radar and unable to get a visual sighting, Gilmore held his course for a few minutes until *Hayasaki* loomed out of the night. He shouted, "Left full rudder" and sounded the collision alarm. *Growler* rammed the enemy ship with a terrific crash that crumpled its own bow, heeled the sub over, and knocked most of the crewmen off their feet. The Japanese sprayed *Growler's* bridge with machine gun fire, wounding Gilmore and killing two others. Four crewmen made it down the hatch. Unable to move, Gilmore gave his last order: "Take her down." The heavily damaged *Growler* limped back to Brisbane 11 days later.

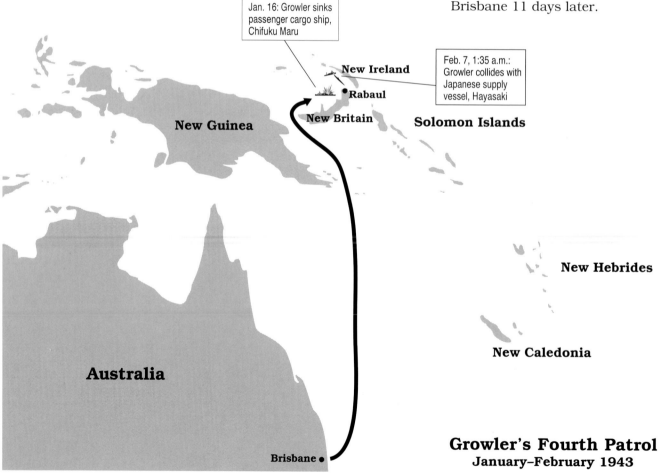

Jan. 16: Growler sinks passenger cargo ship, Chifuku Maru

Feb. 7, 1:35 a.m.: Growler collides with Japanese supply vessel, Hayasaki

New Ireland

Rabaul

New Guinea

New Britain

Solomon Islands

New Hebrides

New Caledonia

Australia

Brisbane •

Growler's Fourth Patrol
January–February 1943

Growler **with** its crushed bow (below) in Brisbane, Australia in February 1943. Fortunately for the submarine, collision damage was confined to the first 25 feet of non-watertight bow structure in front of the pressure hull. The forward torpedo tubes remained intact and repairs were completed in a Brisbane shipyard. Japanese machine gun bullets put holes in the upper conning tower hatch and electrical cables. After the collision, flooding through these holes short-circuited several of the ship's electrical panels.

Howard Gilmore (right) at the Royal Hawaiian Hotel on Oahu. For sacrificing his life to save *Growler*, he was awarded the Congressional Medal of Honor.

Wahoo

Two weeks after Howard Gilmore left Australia on his last patrol, USS *Wahoo* also sailed from Brisbane. A new captain, Dudley "Mush" Morton assumed command of *Wahoo* with orders to reconnoiter Wewak Anchorage on New Guinea's north coast before proceeding to the Caroline Islands. Mush Morton was a supremely aggressive officer, beloved by his crew, and filled with confidence in himself and his ship.

Once at sea, however, Morton couldn't find Wewak on the standard charts. Its location remained a mystery until a member of the crew found it in his recently purchased Australian high school atlas. Now on course, Captain Morton decided that "reconnoiter" meant enter the harbor and attack any ships, and on the morning of January 24, 1943 he did just that. Running submerged into the nine-mile-long anchorage at 3 knots, he spotted a Japanese destroyer. Before he could find a firing solution, the destroyer got underway and headed toward *Wahoo*. Morton quickly fired three torpedoes but all missed astern. He launched two more torpedoes and again they missed. Finally, with the destroyer filling the periscope he fired his sixth torpedo at 750 yards. It hit and blew off the warship's bow. Dodging aerial bombs, a thankful *Wahoo* escaped from the anchorage.

Wahoo topped this exploit two days later when it sank a Japanese transport and three freighters in a troop convoy during a 14-hour sea battle.

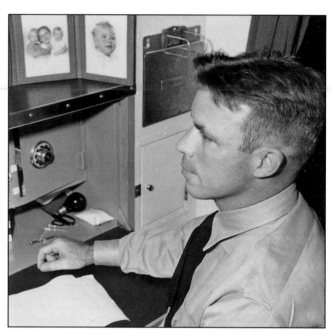

Lt. Comdr. Mush Morton (right) aboard *Wahoo*. He graduated from Annapolis in 1930 and commanded submarine *R-5* in the Atlantic before taking command of *Wahoo* in January 1943.

***Wahoo* leaves** dock at Mare Island (below). *Wahoo*'s executive officer, Richard O'Kane, and third officer, George Grider, would go on to become famous submarine commanders of their own ships: *Tang* and *Flasher*.

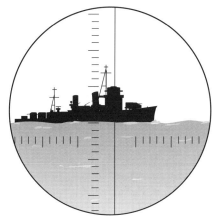

The destroyer, *Harusame* (left), torpedoed by *Wahoo* at Wewak anchorage. Commanded by Captain Masao Kamiyama, the destroyer had spent the previous six months fighting in the Guadalcanal campaign as part of the Tokyo Express supply route. *Harusame* also led the Japanese ship column during the violent night battle off Guadalcanal on October 13, 1942. The Japanese salvaged *Harusame* from Wewak and returned it to duty only to see it sunk by U.S. planes on June 8, 1944.

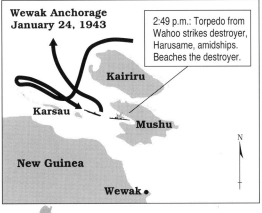

**Wewak Anchorage
January 24, 1943**

2:49 p.m.: Torpedo from Wahoo strikes destroyer, Harusame, amidships. Beaches the destroyer.

Kairiru

Karsau

Mushu

New Guinea

N

Wewak •

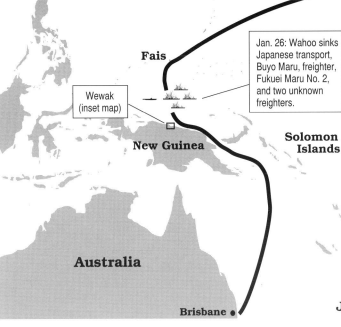

Wake

Hawaiian Islands

Fais

Jan. 26: Wahoo sinks Japanese transport, Buyo Maru, freighter, Fukuei Maru No. 2, and two unknown freighters.

Marshall Islands

Wewak (inset map)

New Guinea

Solomon Islands

Australia

Brisbane •

**Wahoo's Third Patrol
January 16–February 7 1943**

Wahoo's **third** patrol electrified the submarine service. Mush Morton not only torpedoed a veteran Japanese destroyer inside an enemy harbor, he also wiped out a convoy bringing reinforcements to the Imperial Army on New Guinea. Captain Morton received a Navy Cross and *Wahoo* a Presidential Unit Citation for the patrol.

The Yellow Sea

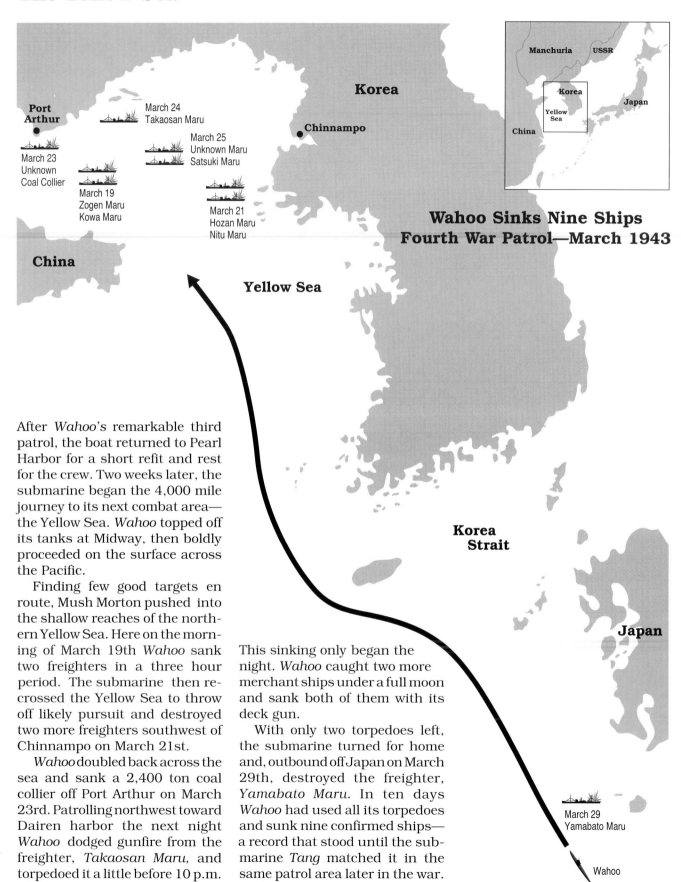

Port Arthur

March 23
Unknown
Coal Collier

March 24
Takaosan Maru

March 19
Zogen Maru
Kowa Maru

March 25
Unknown Maru
Satsuki Maru

March 21
Hozan Maru
Nitu Maru

Korea

Chinnampo

China

Yellow Sea

**Wahoo Sinks Nine Ships
Fourth War Patrol—March 1943**

Manchuria **USSR**

Korea

**Yellow
Sea**

China

Japan

**Korea
Strait**

Japan

March 29
Yamabato Maru

Wahoo

After *Wahoo's* remarkable third patrol, the boat returned to Pearl Harbor for a short refit and rest for the crew. Two weeks later, the submarine began the 4,000 mile journey to its next combat area— the Yellow Sea. *Wahoo* topped off its tanks at Midway, then boldly proceeded on the surface across the Pacific.

Finding few good targets en route, Mush Morton pushed into the shallow reaches of the northern Yellow Sea. Here on the morning of March 19th *Wahoo* sank two freighters in a three hour period. The submarine then recrossed the Yellow Sea to throw off likely pursuit and destroyed two more freighters southwest of Chinnampo on March 21st.

Wahoo doubled back across the sea and sank a 2,400 ton coal collier off Port Arthur on March 23rd. Patrolling northwest toward Dairen harbor the next night *Wahoo* dodged gunfire from the freighter, *Takaosan Maru,* and torpedoed it a little before 10 p.m.

This sinking only began the night. *Wahoo* caught two more merchant ships under a full moon and sank both of them with its deck gun.

With only two torpedoes left, the submarine turned for home and, outbound off Japan on March 29th, destroyed the freighter, *Yamabato Maru.* In ten days *Wahoo* had used all its torpedoes and sunk nine confirmed ships— a record that stood until the submarine *Tang* matched it in the same patrol area later in the war.

The Nitu Maru (above) and a Seiwa Maru-class freighter (right) torpedoed by *Wahoo*. The Japanese expanded their merchant tonnage by one-third in the late 1930s. They believed this fleet adequate to fight a short war with America. The shock of defeat at Guadalcanal in December 1942 forced them to make merchant vessel construction a priority. By 1944 cargo ship-building increased six times over the 1941 level, but U.S. submarines sank twice as many merchant ships as the Empire produced. Inability to import raw materials past the submarine blockade forced the Japanese economy to a halt in the last year of the war. Mush Morton and *Wahoo* accelerated this process and set a new standard for the submarine force. In 60 days *Wahoo* sank 12 enemy merchant ships and one fleet destroyer.

Depth Charged!

The day *Wahoo* began its rampage in the Yellow Sea (March 19th), USS *Kingfish*, 800 miles to the south in the East China Sea, torpedoed and sank a large Japanese troop transport which carried reinforcements to the Philippines. *Kingfish* escaped immediate counterattack, but retribution was not long in coming.

Four days later at 3 a.m. the sub ran into a Japanese destroyer which forced it to dive, rig ship for silent running, and begin evasive action. In the East China Sea's shallow 350-foot depth, the destroyer easily maintained sound contact and began a bitter seven hour depth charge attack.

Although the close explosions broke lights, stopped gauges, and forced open numerous hull valves, the damage remained minor until the last attack at 12:27 p.m. Two depth charges of a string of six exploded within 40 feet of *Kingfish's* stern and sent three tremendous shock waves through the ship. The vibrations knocked men down, threw them out of their bunks, and dished in the hull surrounding the forward engine room. For the next six hours the submarine lay on the bottom, making emergency repairs. After dark *Kingfish* and its grateful crew surfaced and began the journey back to Pearl Harbor.

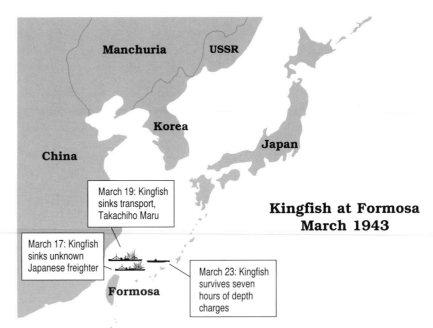

March 19: Kingfish sinks transport, Takachiho Maru

March 17: Kingfish sinks unknown Japanese freighter

March 23: Kingfish survives seven hours of depth charges

Kingfish at Formosa March 1943

A transport (right) sunk by *Kingfish.* Captain Vernon Lawrence torpedoed the 8,000 ton troopship, *Takachiho Maru,* after decoding an Ultra dispatch which gave its position.

***Kingfish* at Mare** Island after overhaul (below). The submarine completed 12 war patrols and officially sank 14 Japanese ships, including three tankers.

Depth-charging of Kingfish
March 23, 1943
4:48 A.M.–12:27 P.M.

Japanese Destroyer

Kingfish

Water Depth
350 ft.

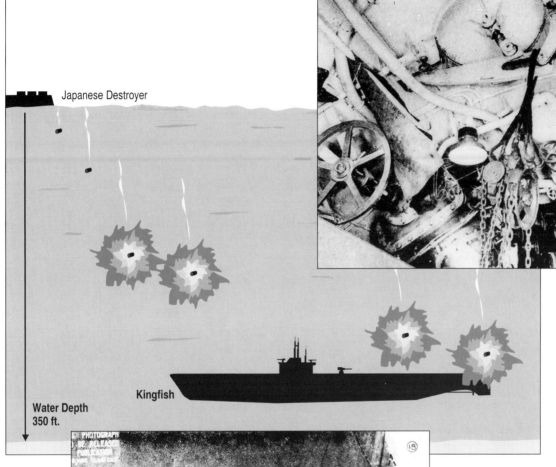

temporary repairs at Pearl Harbor, the submarine proceeded to Mare Island Navy Yard for extensive over-haul. Navy work-men found severe damage in the engine rooms (above) and the after torpedo room, where the pressure hull's circularity had been distorted. Numerous dents pockmarked the hull (left). The explosions ripped off the torpedo loading skid and bent the star-board propeller. Both periscope prisms shattered and one periscope tube flooded. Blasts tore off one sound head and twisted the other. It took Mare Island eight weeks to repair Kingfish and return the ship to duty.

When the last two depth charges forced Kingfish to the bottom, the crew prepared to scuttle the ship if necessary. Men destroyed the coding machine and disabled the Torpedo Data Computer, while other sailors plugged major leaks in both engine rooms. Kingfish surfaced after dark, how-ever, evading the Japanese, and limped home. After

69

Solemn Victory

During the first year of the war, the U.S. Navy lost eight submarines. The bitter fighting in the Solomon Islands would soon increase the toll. Although the Japanese retreated from Guadalcanal in January 1943, they were determined to retain the rest of the Solomons and New Guinea. Their navy brought heavily-escorted convoys into Rabaul to reinforce garrisons in the Solomons.

The new commander of U.S. submarines in Brisbane, Commodore James Fife was equally determined to attack these convoys to prepare the way for Operation Cartwheel, the Allied strategic offensive to take northern New Guinea and the Solomons. Using Ultra information about enemy ship locations, he planned to direct his subs by radio from Australia: "play checkers" with his boats to increase the "bag" of enemy ships. Unfortunately this tactic entailed a dramatic increase in radio traffic which betrayed the submarines' locations to the Japanese.

On January 10, 1943 Fife ordered *Argonaut* to assault a convoy escorted by three destroyers. The submarine attacked, but the Japanese forced *Argonaut* to the surface and sank the sub. A few weeks later, *Amberjack* and *Grampus* vanished in the Solomons after making radio transmissions to Brisbane. Japanese destroyers sank another Brisbane submarine, *Triton*, on March 15th. In a little over two months the U.S. lost four veteran boats, carrying 319 submariners.

Commodore James Fife (below) presenting the Presidential Unit Citation to a submarine in August 1943. Although the Navy exonerated Fife in an investigation after the loss of four subs under his command, some officers criticized him for requiring too many radio contacts from his submarines.

April 1943 — ▦ Japanese-occupied

**Operation Cartwheel
Allied Strategic Offensive Plan**

Triton (left) departed Brisbane on February 16, 1943 on its sixth war patrol. Capt. G. K. McKenzie sank one freighter and damaged another on March 6th. Nine days later, three patrolling Japanese destroyers located and depth-charged *Triton*. The entire crew went down with the ship.

On its third war patrol *Amberjack* (below) shelled a schooner and attacked a munitions ship, Anti-submarine forces sank the boat on February 16, 1943.

Triton
March 15, 1943

Admiralty Is.

New Ireland

Rabaul •

New Britain

Amberjack
Feb. 16, 1943

Argonaut
Jan. 10, 1943

Bougainville

Solomon Islands

New Guinea

Grampus
Feb/March 1943

Guadalcanal

Grampus (below) sailed on its sixth war patrol on February 11, 1943. Apart from a radio message the next day, no word was ever received from the submarine. Two destroyers may have sunk it in Blackett Strait on March 5th.

Australia

Argonaut (left) at sea. After the Makin Island raid the submarine went to Brisbane to conduct special missions for Gen. MacArthur. Commodore Fife, however, believed *Argonaut* could make a regular war patrol and he sent the old sub into the hazardous waters off New Britain. There, on January 10, 1943, he ordered *Argonaut* to attack a five ship convoy escorted by three destroyers. By chance a passing U.S. plane saw the submarine's last battle. After damaging one destroyer by torpedo, the other two attacked and forced *Argonaut* to the surface. They sank the sub with gunfire. One hundred and five men went down with the ship.

71

New Weapons

In the summer of 1943 new weapons increased the offensive power of U.S. submarines. Surface radar was the most important innovation. Developed by the Western Electric Company, submarine SJ radar could locate enemy ships and planes at a distance of 8–12 miles and give their direction and range. The SJ radar mast mounted on the conning tower extended the submarine's ability to detect, track, and destroy Japanese shipping, especially with high-speed night surface attacks.

Once near a convoy on the surface, the commander used his Target Bearing Transmitter (TBT), a pair of rotating binoculars attached to a gyro compass-repeater on the bridge, to transfer course, range, and bearing to the Torpedo Data Computer in the control room. The Torpedo Data Computer (TDC) electromechanically processed this information and calculated a firing solution. The computer then automatically set the gyro angles on the torpedoes in the tubes.

The submarine fired newly-developed Mark 18 electric torpedoes which, while slower than the Mark 14 steam torpedoes, left no wake for enemy escorts to track. After the attack, the submarine dived to elude the escorts. The bathothermograph, on the sub's conning tower, detected thermoclines. These colder layers of water deflected enemy sonar beams, allowing the submarine to escape.

The Approach

Upon sighting a distant ship, the submarine swung toward it to establish its general direction. If the target's track allowed an attack, the submarine set an intercept course. The goal was to pull ahead of the enemy ship and wait in ambush within torpedo range until it arrived.

1. SJ Radar detected an enemy ship and plotted its course and range.

SJ Radar

2. The commander on the bridge used the TBT to determine enemy bearing and angle-on-the-bow.

Target Bearing Transmitter (TBT)

3. **Torpedo Data Computer (TDC).** Once within firing range, the TDC used course, range, bearing, and angle-on-the-bow estimates to compute gyro angle settings for the torpedoes.

The Attack

angle-on-the-bow to input into the Torpedo Data Computer. The TDC then calculated the enemy vessel's course and speed, and adjusted the torpedoes' gyros to run a converging course. If the target did not maneuver away and the torpedoes ran "hot, straight, and true," they struck the ship and exploded.

When the sub approached a ship, the commander made a series of quick periscope observations of the target's range and

4. The submarine fired Mark 18 electric torpedoes, which left no wake.

Mark 18 Torpedo

5. While the sub dived, the bathothermograph on the conning tower sensed temperature differentials in the water. The sub evaded enemy sonar by hiding beneath a layer of cool water.

Cool layer of water

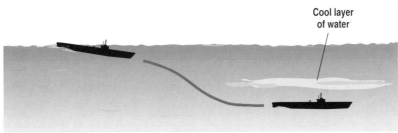

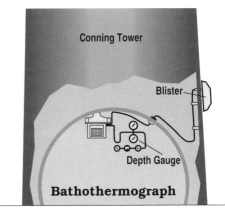

Conning Tower

Blister

Depth Gauge

Bathothermograph

Wahoo's Last Patrol

After *Wahoo's* spectacular fourth patrol, Captain Mush Morton took the submarine to the Aleutians to cover the American attack on Attu Island. Although faulty Mark 14 torpedoes plagued the voyage, *Wahoo* sank three Japanese cargo ships in early May before returning to Pearl Harbor, and then to California for an overhaul.

Wahoo came back from refit in August 1943 in time to join *Plunger* on the second American submarine foray into the Sea of Japan. Once again most of the Mark 14 steam torpedoes on both submarines malfunctioned. After firing ten duds in a row *Wahoo* returned to Pearl Harbor to replace the remaining torpedoes. An exasperated Morton convinced Admiral Lockwood to let him go back to the Sea of Japan with a load of new Mark 18 electric torpedoes.

Wahoo sailed from Pearl Harbor on its seventh war patrol on September 9, 1943. The sub topped off the tanks at Midway and proceeded west with orders to enter the Sea of Japan via La Perouse Strait around September 20th and patrol below the 43rd parallel for four weeks. Pearl Harbor ordered another U.S. submarine, *Sawfish,* to enter the Sea of Japan three days later and patrol above that parallel. If all went well *Wahoo* would depart the area on October 21st.

Wahoo, Mush Morton, and 79 crew members left Midway on September 13th and never returned. A study of Japanese records after the war revealed the submarine's fate. Between September 29th and October 9th *Wahoo* sank four ships in the Sea of Japan, including the 8,000 ton *Konron Maru.*

While on patrol, *Wahoo* sustained damage from unknown causes. Post-war studies of the Mark 18 torpedo revealed a tendency to circle back on the boat that fired it. This may have happened to *Wahoo.* In any event, the submarine was leaking oil when it attempted to pass through La Perouse Strait on the morning of October 11, 1943. Japanese coastal artillery sighted the sub and opened fire. *Wahoo* dived but the Japanese began a series of coordinated air and sea attacks near the telltale oil slick. A barrage of depth charges shortly after noon ended the submarine's life.

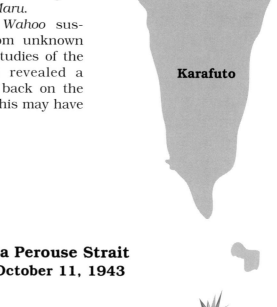

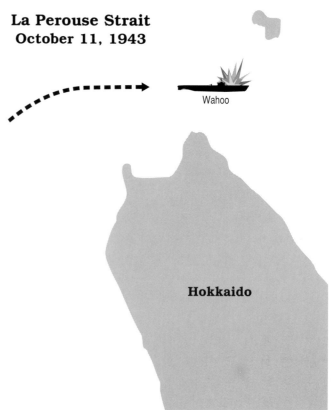

La Perouse Strait
October 11, 1943

Wahoo

Wahoo's 7th War Patrol
September–October 1943

74

9:45 A.M. Zero drops two bombs on *Wahoo*. Oil rises to the surface.

12:07 P.M. Japanese sub chaser reaches the site and drops 16 depth charges on *Wahoo*.

Wahoo's **last** battle (left opposite and above) as reconstructed from Japanese war records. It was postulated after the war that *Wahoo* may have been damaged by a circular run of one of its own defective Mark 18 electric torpedoes. Such damage would explain why Captain Morton chose to make the passage through La Perouse Strait on the surface in daylight. In any case, a large-caliber coast artillery gun on Soya Misaki promontory sighted *Wahoo* around

8:30 a.m. on October 11, 1943 and opened fire. The submarine submerged and continued on course. The Japanese battery commander alerted patrol aircraft and ships to the intruder's presence. An hour later, a patrol seaplane arrived and spotted a small oil slick on the water. Closer inspection revealed a submerged black hull and conning tower. This seaplane and another dropped several bombs on the target and brought up bubbles and oil. At noon a submarine chaser

arrived and dropped 16 depth charges, bringing up one of *Wahoo's* propeller blades. After this barrage the Japanese could not find the submarine. Only an expanding oil slick of diesel fuel 200 feet wide and three miles long marked *Wahoo's* grave.

Commander Dudley "Mush" Morton (right) was awarded a fourth Navy Cross posthumously for *Wahoo's* seventh and final patrol. He received official credit for sinking 19 Japanese ships while captain of the *Wahoo*.

Into the East China Sea

Two outstanding submarine patrols in the fall of 1943—the first by *Seahorse* and the second by *Bowfin*—demonstrated how effective the war on Japanese merchant shipping had become. *Seahorse's* patrol began on October 20, 1943 when the boat left Midway for the East China Sea. Lt. Comdr. Slade Cutter, a former Naval Academy football star, ran the submarine with a mixture of discipline and informality that earned him the respect and admiration of his crew. On its way into the patrol area *Seahorse* sank three fishing trawlers with its deck gun. Cutter, however, disliked attacking these small unarmed vessels and ordered the practice stopped.

Worthier targets showed up around midnight on October 31st when radar detected a large 20-ship convoy south of Japan. In a running two day battle, *Seahorse* torpedoed and sank the 7,000 ton *Chihaya Maru* and 5,800 ton *Ume Maru.* Submarines, *Trigger* and *Halibut,* also attacked the same convoy and sank three ships.

Seahorse continued on patrol, but bad luck and alert escorts foiled several more attacks until November 22nd. On that clear night, Cutter maneuvered past three destroyers and sank the 3,300 ton freighter, *Daishu Maru.* Four days later, at midnight, the submarine intercepted two ships fleeing into the safety of Tsushima Strait. With four remarkable two-mile-long torpedo shots *Seahorse* sank them both. Now out of ammunition, the submarine left the East China Sea on December 1st, having sunk 27,000 tons of Japanese shipping.

U.S.S. SEAHORSE (SS-304)

Captain Slade Cutter and the crew of *Seahorse* (top) after sinking four ships off Luzon on the submarine's fifth war patrol.

Seahorse's **logo** (above). U.S. submariners often created emblems of the sea creatures for which their ships were named.

USS *Seahorse* (right) in 1945. Slade Cutter was the executive officer on the submarine's first war patrol. He assumed command on the second voyage and sank five ships in the East China Sea. Over the next eight months and three patrols *Seahorse* sank an additional 14 ships, including the Japanese submarine, *RO-45*.

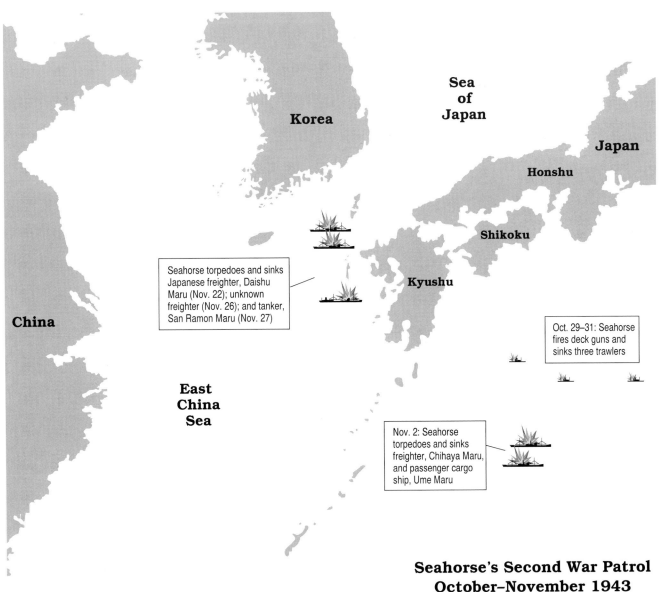

Seahorse torpedoes and sinks Japanese freighter, Daishu Maru (Nov. 22); unknown freighter (Nov. 26); and tanker, San Ramon Maru (Nov. 27)

Oct. 29–31: Seahorse fires deck guns and sinks three trawlers

Nov. 2: Seahorse torpedoes and sinks freighter, Chihaya Maru, and passenger cargo ship, Ume Maru

Korea

Sea of Japan

Japan

Honshu

Shikoku

Kyushu

China

East China Sea

**Seahorse's Second War Patrol
October–November 1943**

Bowfin

One day before *Seahorse* and *Trigger* mauled a large Japanese convoy in the East China Sea (November 2, 1943), *Bowfin* left Australia and headed north on its second war patrol. The submarine's new commander, Walter T. Griffith, was determined to attack every Japanese target his ship could find.

Griffith's first chance came on November 9th when *Bowfin* used its deck gun to sink four schooners. Two nights later, the submarine caught two small oil tankers in Sibutu Passage near Borneo and once again destroyed them in a gun action. After that targets became scarce and *Bowfin* took station with *Billfish* off the coast of Indochina on November 20th.

A gale arose, and in the heavy seas, rain, and wind the two submarines lost contact. During the black night of November 26th *Bowfin's* faulty SJ radar suddenly gave contacts at 1,000 and 4,000 yards. A large tanker loomed out

of the rain and Griffith realized his submarine was in the middle of a five-ship enemy convoy. Crashing through the rough seas, on the surface, *Bowfin* torpedoed and sank the 5,000 ton *Ogurasan Maru* and the 5,400 ton freighter, *Tainan Maru*. Only gasoline, burning on the water marked the two ships' graves when the submarine cleared the scene to reload. The weary fire control party on *Bowfin* sighted another ship at 8:30 a.m., and after two hours of difficult tracking, destroyed the transport with four torpedoes.

Continuing its lucky streak the next morning, *Bowfin* sank a pro-German Vichy French coastal steamer, *Van Vollenhoven*. Eight hours later, Captain Griffith received a signal from *Billfish* that reported another five-ship convoy nearby. *Bowfin* approached the merchantmen on the surface, and in poor visibility at 3:15 a.m., sank the cargo ship, *Sydney Maru*, and the tanker, *Tonan Maru*. One

Bowfin (above) began its career on September 25, 1943 when it destroyed its first enemy ship, the large 8,000 ton transport, *Kirishima Maru*, off the coast of Indochina. Over the next six months, under the command of Captain Walter T. Griffith, the submarine sank nine more ships. *Bowfin* ended the war as part of the submarine wolf pack that broke into the Sea of Japan in June 1945 and sank 28 ships.

of the surviving ships sighted the sub and opened fire with a five-inch deck gun. The second shell hit *Bowfin* and shattered part of the main induction valve. Griffith fired stern torpedoes into the attacking freighter. Both exploded and the gunfire ceased as the ship went down. A repair crew patched *Bowfin's* damage well enough to allow the sub to dive.

Back in Fremantle, Griffith received a Navy Cross and *Bowfin* a Presidential Unit Citation. Together *Bowfin*, *Seahorse*, and 30 other U.S. submarines sank a record 62 ships in November 1943.

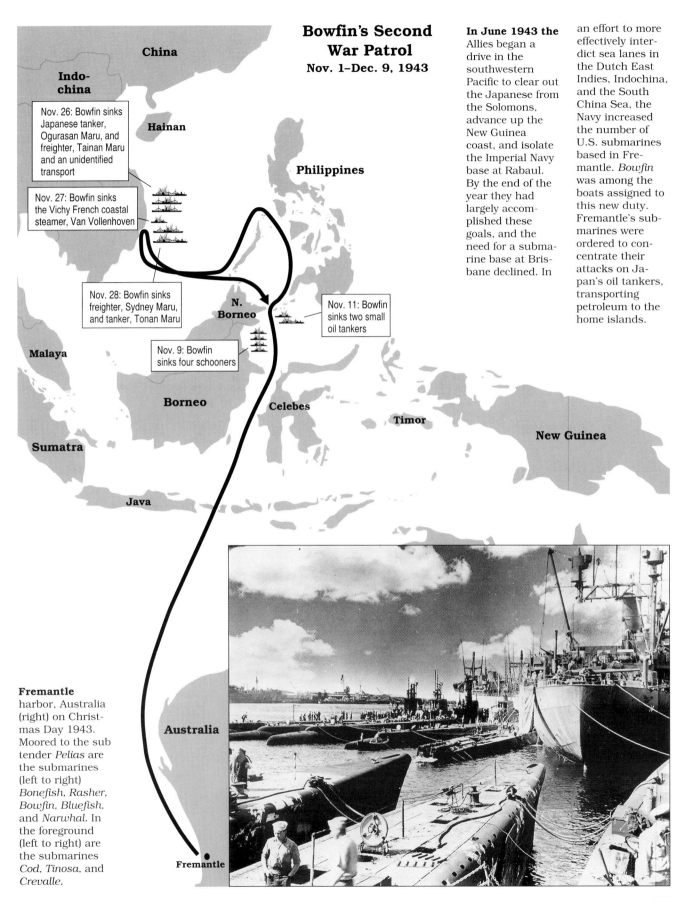

Bowfin's Second War Patrol
Nov. 1–Dec. 9, 1943

China

Indo-china

Nov. 26: Bowfin sinks Japanese tanker, Ogurasan Maru, and freighter, Tainan Maru and an unidentified transport

Hainan

Nov. 27: Bowfin sinks the Vichy French coastal steamer, Van Vollenhoven

Philippines

Nov. 28: Bowfin sinks freighter, Sydney Maru, and tanker, Tonan Maru

N. Borneo

Nov. 11: Bowfin sinks two small oil tankers

Malaya

Nov. 9: Bowfin sinks four schooners

Borneo

Celebes

Timor

New Guinea

Sumatra

Java

Fremantle harbor, Australia (right) on Christmas Day 1943. Moored to the sub tender *Pelias* are the submarines (left to right) *Bonefish, Rasher, Bowfin, Bluefish,* and *Narwhal.* In the foreground (left to right) are the submarines *Cod, Tinosa,* and *Crevalle.*

Australia

Fremantle

In June 1943 the Allies began a drive in the southwestern Pacific to clear out the Japanese from the Solomons, advance up the New Guinea coast, and isolate the Imperial Navy base at Rabaul. By the end of the year they had largely accomplished these goals, and the need for a submarine base at Brisbane declined. In an effort to more effectively interdict sea lanes in the Dutch East Indies, Indochina, and the South China Sea, the Navy increased the number of U.S. submarines based in Fremantle. *Bowfin* was among the boats assigned to this new duty. Fremantle's submarines were ordered to concentrate their attacks on Japan's oil tankers, transporting petroleum to the home islands.

Invasion of the Gilbert Islands

At the Trident Conference in May 1943 the U.S. Joint Chiefs of Staff decided that the main offensive against Japan should be through the atolls of the central Pacific: the Gilberts, Marshalls, and Marianas islands. They also ordered General MacArthur to continue his secondary advance in the Solomons and New Guinea.

By the fall of 1943, production miracles at American shipyards gave the U.S. Navy the necessary aircraft carriers, battleships, cruisers, destroyers, and transports to organize Operation Galvanic, a powerful amphibious invasion of the Gilbert Islands. That assault came on the morning of November 20, 1943 when the Second Marine Division stormed two-mile-long Betio Island at the southern end of Tarawa Atoll. Their landing hampered by low tides, the Marines suffered numerous casualties as 4,000 entrenched Japanese defenders fought to the death.

Meanwhile, Admiral Lockwood assigned a dozen submarines to support Operation Galvanic. *Nautilus*, which carried Carlson's raiders to Makin Island 15 months before, was ordered to ferry a 78-man Marine reconnaissance company to the lightly defended island of Abemama, 76 miles south of Tarawa. On the way, the U.S. destroyer, *Ringgold*, attacked *Nautilus* in spite of its frantic recognition signals, and put a 5-inch shell (which fortunately failed to explode) into the sub's conning tower. *Nautilus* dived to escape and the next night landed the Marines, who subsequently captured Abemama Island.

The submarine *Corvina*, on its first war patrol, helped to blockade Truk. On November 16th the Japanese submarine *I-176* caught *Corvina* on the surface and torpedoed it with a loss of all hands.

The Marines captured Tarawa after three bloody days of fighting at a cost of 3,300 casualties.

U.S. Marines (below) storm a bombproof Japanese blockhouse on Tarawa. The U.S. seizure of Tarawa in the Gilbert Islands marked the beginning of the central Pacific offensive, modeled on the old War Plan Orange. The attack pitted 18,000 U.S. 2nd Division Marines against 4,000 Imperial Marines of the Sasebo 7th Special Naval Landing Force.

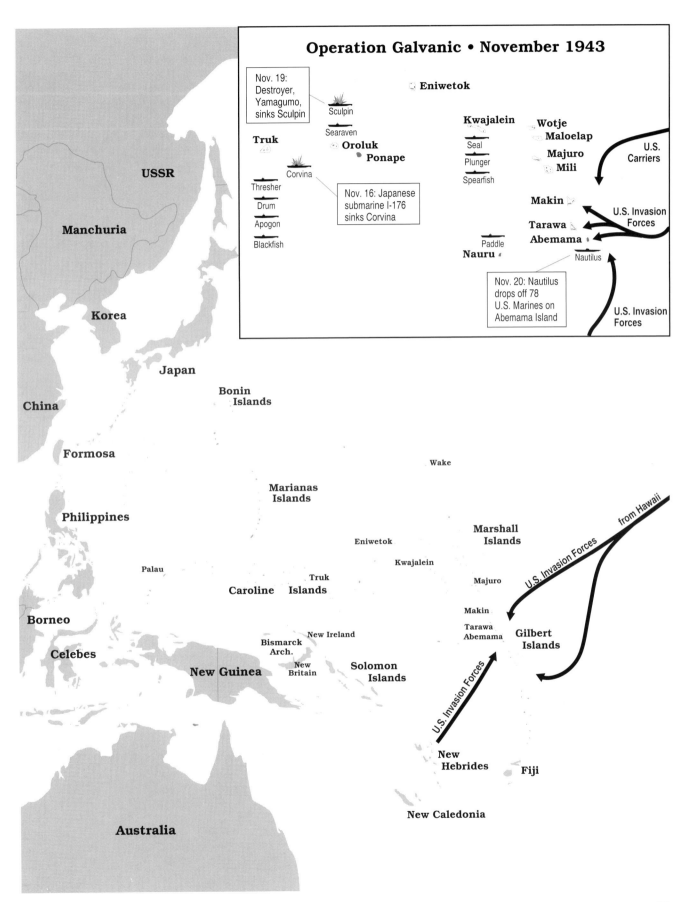

Operation Galvanic • November 1943

Nov. 19: Destroyer, Yamagumo, sinks Sculpin

Sculpin

Searaven

Eniwetok

Truk

Oroluk

Ponape

Corvina

Thresher

Drum

Apogon

Blackfish

Nov. 16: Japanese submarine I-176 sinks Corvina

Kwajalein

Seal

Plunger

Spearfish

Wotje

Maloelap

Majuro

Mili

Makin

Tarawa

Abemama

Paddle

Nauru

Nautilus

Nov. 20: Nautilus drops off 78 U.S. Marines on Abemama Island

U.S. Carriers

U.S. Invasion Forces

U.S. Invasion Forces

USSR

Manchuria

Korea

China

Japan

Bonin Islands

Formosa

Wake

Marianas Islands

Philippines

Eniwetok

Kwajalein

Palau

Truk

Caroline Islands

Marshall Islands

Majuro

Makin

Tarawa

Abemama

Gilbert Islands

Borneo

New Ireland

Bismarck Arch.

Celebes

New Guinea

New Britain

Solomon Islands

U.S. Invasion Forces

from Hawaii

U.S. Invasion Forces

New Hebrides

Fiji

New Caledonia

Australia

Medal of Honor

Corvina was not the only U.S. submarine lost in support of Operation Galvanic. *Sculpin* left Pearl Harbor on November 5, 1943 to patrol east of Truk and intercept any Japanese reinforcements headed for Tarawa or Makin Island. Besides its skipper, Fred Connaway, *Sculpin* carried senior officer, John P. Cromwell, to direct a wolf pack against Japanese relief convoys. Cromwell knew the details of Operation Galvanic as well as the use of Ultra to decipher Japanese plans.

Sculpin reached its station, and on the night of November 18th, detected a large Japanese convoy sailing from Truk to reinforce the Marshall Islands. The submarine circled ahead of the convoy at high speed for a dawn attack, but escorts spotted its periscope and forced the boat down before *Sculpin* could fire torpedoes. The sub stayed deep for an hour, and then after a quick periscope observation, surfaced to pursue the enemy ships.

Unfortunately for *Sculpin*, the Japanese anticipated this tactic and left the destroyer *Yamagumo* silently waiting three miles from the submarine's position. The warship raced toward the sub, forcing it back under. Exploding depth charges caused leaks and damaged several depth gauges aboard *Sculpin*. *Yamagumo* delivered two more accurate depth charge attacks which caused further flooding. Around 10:30 a.m. the temporary diving officer, misled by shattered depth gauges, broached the submarine to the surface and brought *Sculpin* another punishing depth-charging. Repair parties reported severe damage to the torpedo tubes and steering gear. Conditions aboard *Sculpin* deteriorated from flooding, intense heat from the previous night's high-speed run and a low battery charge. After a fourth jarring depth charge attack at 12:30 p.m. Commander Connaway decided *Sculpin's* only chance was to fight the destroyer with the deck gun while the crew abandoned ship.

USS *Sculpin* (below) began the war as part of the U.S. Asiatic Fleet, defending the Philippines. The submarine conducted nine war patrols and received official credit for sinking three Japanese ships before it was sunk off of Oroluk in the Caroline Islands.

Captain John Cromwell (right) went aboard *Sculpin* to coordinate the three-submarine wolf pack of *Sculpin*, *Searaven*, and *Apogon*. Pearl Harbor ordered the group formed on November 29th but *Sculpin*, scuttled ten days earlier, never answered.

The submarine surfaced at 1 p.m. and opened fire. Its three-inch gun proved no match for *Yamagumo's* multiple five-inch guns. Within minutes the Japanese gunners found the range. Two shells hit the conning tower and killed Commander Connaway and most of the gun crew. Surviving officer, Lt. George Brown, ordered the crew to abandon ship. Unwilling to risk capture because of his knowledge of Allied plans, Captain John Cromwell decided go down with the sub.

Sculpin sank at 1:15 p.m. on November 19, 1943. The Japanese picked up 41 survivors. The Navy posthumously awarded John Cromwell the Medal of Honor.

The Congressional Medal of Honor

General George Washington established the first American military decoration, the Purple Heart, in 1782 during the Revolutionary War. At the outbreak of the Civil War in 1861, the U.S. Congress authorized a medal of honor for the Navy and the Army.

The Medal of Honor is the highest decoration of the U.S. Armed Forces. Congress awards the medal for bravery at the risk of life above and beyond the call of duty. Seven U.S. submariners won the Medal of Honor during World War II: the first went to Lt. Comdr. Howard Gilmore of the *Growler;* the second to Capt. John P. Cromwell who went down with *Sculpin;* the third to Capt. Lawson "Red" Ramage of the submarine *Parche;* the fourth to Capt. Samuel Dealey of *Harder;* the fifth to Capt. Gene Fluckey of *Barb;* the sixth to Capt. George Street of *Tirante;* and the seventh to Richard O' Kane of *Tang.*

7:30 A.M.   **Nov. 19, 1943**

Sculpin surfaces and finds the Japanese destroyer, *Yamagumo,* lying in wait. *Sculpin* dives and the destroyer drops depth charges.

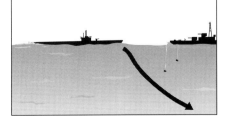

10:30 A.M.

Sculpin's depth gage sticks and the submarine accidentally broaches, revealing its position. *Yamagumo* begins a new round of depth charges.

1:00 P.M.

Sculpin surfaces to fight it out and is hit by destroyer gunfire. The crew scuttles the sub and abandons ship. Commander Connaway is killed. Captain Cromwell goes down with *Sculpin.*

Sister Ships

On November 28, 1943, at Truk, the Japanese divided *Sculpin's* 41 surviving crewmen into two groups and loaded them aboard the aircraft carriers, *Chuyo* and *Unyo*. Escorted by the light carrier, *Zuiho*, the cruiser, *Maya*, and two destroyers, the convoy left Truk lagoon and set course for Japan.

Five days later on December 3rd, *Sailfish*, *Sculpin's* sister ship, surfaced 300 miles southeast of Tokyo in typhoon weather. Tremendous seas, driven by 50 knot winds, lashed the bridge and reduced visibility to a few hundred yards. Just before midnight *Sailfish* picked up a convoy on radar and Lt. Comdr. Robert Ward realized his ship was on the left flank of a fast group of Japanese warships heading northwest. *Sailfish* dived to 40 feet and fired four torpedoes at the biggest ship only 2,100 yards away. Two minutes later, one or two of the torpedoes hit the carrier *Chuyo*. The submarine went deep to reload its tubes and crossed astern of the damaged ship. *Sailfish* surfaced after two hours and commenced a slow approach through the mountainous seas, toward the slowly moving target.

At dawn, with visibility improving rapidly, *Sailfish* fired four torpedoes at *Chuyo* but only one

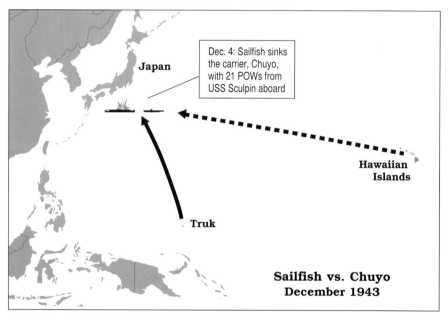

Dec. 4: Sailfish sinks the carrier, Chuyo, with 21 POWs from USS Sculpin aboard

Japan

Hawaiian Islands

Truk

**Sailfish vs. Chuyo
December 1943**

hit. Just after 9 a.m the submarine closed the target again and Lt. Comdr. Ward watched *Chuyo* through the periscope, noting "many planes on deck forward and enough people on deck aft to populate a fair-sized village." Finally, at 9:40 a.m., *Sailfish* fired three more torpedoes at *Chuyo* and scored two more hits. The submarine's crew heard "exceptionally loud breaking up noises." Six minutes later *Chuyo* rolled on its port side and sank.

Although all 21 of *Sculpin's* survivors aboard *Chuyo* were on deck when the carrier went down,

Sailfish (SS 192) (top) and *Sculpin* (SS 191) were sister ships built in the Portsmouth Navy Yard at the same time. *Sailfish*, formerly *Squalus*, foundered off the coast of New Hampshire during a test dive in May 1939 and *Sculpin* assisted in the rescue of the crew. Ironically, *Sailfish* later became the agent for loss of part of *Sculpin's* crew.

the Japanese escort rescued only one American from the water, leaving the rest to drown. It was not until the occupation of Japan at the end of the war that the tragic rendezvous of *Sculpin's* survivors and its sister ship *Sailfish* became known.

I began taking in water. I looked up, saw light, and no longer felt suction—an air pocket must have pushed me upwards. I made one last effort and broke the surface.

—George Rocek
USS *Sculpin*

During *Sculpin's* last fight, when Motor Machinist George Rocek heard the order to abandon ship, he hurried topside. Although stunned by a direct hit on the conning tower, he managed to jump overboard. From the water, he watched *Sculpin* submerge for the last time, and felt the explosions of the boat's batteries. The destroyer, *Yamagumo,* picked up 41 *Sculpin* survivors. The Japanese tied up the wounded, shocked, and oil-covered men and left them on deck during the stormy trip back to Truk.

At Truk, the POWs endured constant interrogations and brutal beatings on only a few ounces of rice and very little water. After ten days, the Japanese divided them into two groups and put them aboard the escort carriers, *Unyo* and *Chuyo* for the voyage back to Japan. They locked Rocek's group of 21 in a small, hot compartment below decks on the carrier *Chuyo.*

At midnight on December 3rd, in the midst of a typhoon, a terrific explosion rocked *Chuyo.* A torpedo from the U.S. submarine *Sailfish* had struck the carrier. *Chuyo* lost power, and smoke filtered into the Americans' compartment. The prisoners heard a Japanese damage control party try to shore up a weakened bulkhead beneath them, but it soon collapsed and water poured into the compartment below. They yelled frantically to the Japanese to let them out but no one came. With the water rising, they pried a metal pump handle off a fixture and broke open the locked hatch. The Americans held onto one another and threaded their way upward through the dark, smoke-filled compartments to the carrier's flight deck. Topside, they found the crew furiously lashing poles together to make rafts.

While they were on deck, another torpedo from *Sailfish* shattered the carrier's port side and *Chuyo* began to capsize. George Rocek slid down the flight deck into the sea. The tremendous suction pulled him under and he realized he was going to drown. Then suddenly, the suction ended and a large air bubble from the carrier lifted him back to the surface, twenty feet from a raft containing two other *Sculpin* survivors.

The nearby Japanese destroyer, fearing submarine attack, circled for five hours in the high winds and huge swells before picking up survivors. The Japanese lowered ropes and a ladder. In the large waves, the ropes were useless. Rocek's only chance was to climb the rope ladder. With his last strength he reached it only to have a Japanese officer step over him and force him back into the sea. Then a large wave lifted him up and deposited him on the ladder. He locked his arms around the ladder just as the Japanese pulled it up and got underway. They did not pick up the other *Sculpin* survivors.

In January 1944, after two more months of interrogation and beatings, the Japanese sent Rocek and the other group of *Sculpin* survivors to the Ashio copper mines. The Allies liberated them in September 1945.

Escort carrier *Chuyo:* 17,000 tons; 550 feet long; carried 27 aircraft.

Grand Escort Force

Japan neglected its vital merchant marine throughout World War II. The Imperial Navy stubbornly overvalued its tradition of offensive warfare and refused to commit the necessary resources to a defensive anti-submarine campaign. The rapid Japanese victories of 1942 reinforced this policy and caused a series of strategic errors in the war at sea.

First, was the failure to organize an Empire-wide convoy system. The naval command assigned a small number of officers to the problem of shipping protection. They were unable to overcome the Combined Fleet's refusal to provide modern destroyers as escorts for ordinary merchant ships. They also encountered resistance from some civilian cargo authorities who wanted their vessels to sail independently rather than in convoys. Despite these problems, the officers' efforts led the Japanese Navy to create a small independent merchant ship escort force in April 1942.

The first escort group consisted of 17 old patrol vessels assigned to cover the Japan–Singapore sealane. The second escort group of seven dated warships received the unenviable task of guarding the route to Truk, Japan's main naval base in the central Pacific. The meager forces available to these escort groups illustrated Japan's second major blunder in its undersea war: failure to build large numbers of patrol vessels.

Before the war, the Imperial Navy built four prototype anti-submarine ships: the *kaikobans*, or coast defense vessels. These small 800 ton, diesel-powered ships were armed with two 4.7-inch guns, 120 depth charges, and could be built in 3–6 months. They were a formidable threat to submarines. With sufficient *kaikobans*, Japan could have protected its merchant fleet. But none were built in 1942, and only 14 in 1943. Not until 1944 did the Japanese launch enough of these vessels to face the experienced,

A Type C *kaikoban* (above) at sea. Japan built 57 out of the 118 planned escort ships. U.S. submarines sank 11 of them; USS *Torsk* torpedoed two on the last day of the war.

Kaikobans were 250 feet long and could reach a top speed of 16 knots. The vessel shown above was *Kaikoban No. 1*. B-24 aircraft attacked and sank it on April 6, 1945 near Formosa.

and technically-advanced U.S. submarine force.

Great shipping losses in the fall of 1943 forced the Japanese High Command to recognize the inadequacy of their convoy escort system. On November 15th they organized the Grand Escort Fleet, consisting of the First and Second Escort forces, and the newly-formed 901 Air Escort Squadron. Still, convoy defense vessels remained last on the list for good radio equipment and the all-important surface radar. Lacking these tools, the Grand Escort Force did not develop the tactics needed to defeat their submarine opponents.

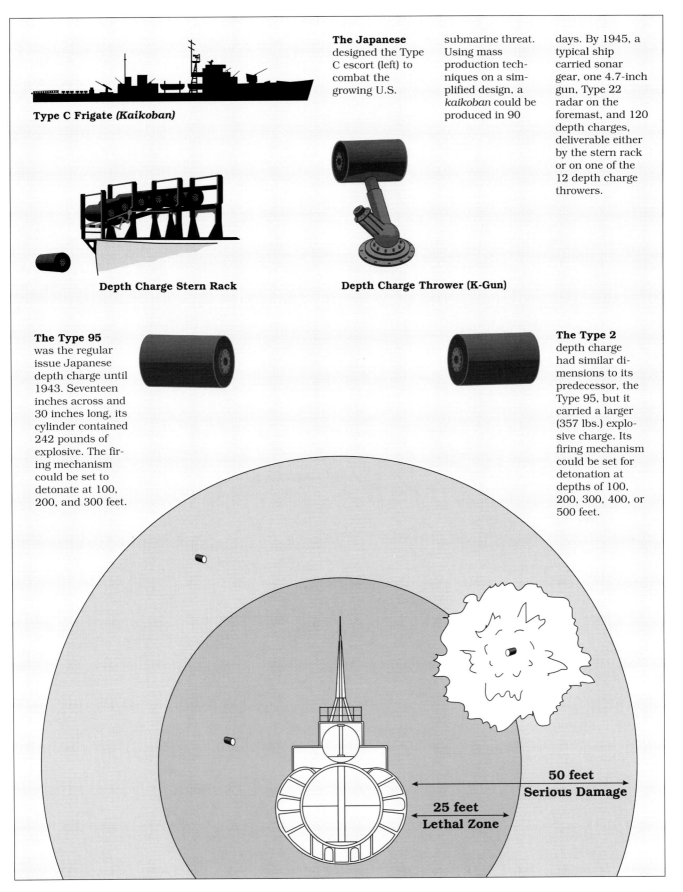

Type C Frigate *(Kaikoban)*

Depth Charge Stern Rack

Depth Charge Thrower (K-Gun)

The Japanese designed the Type C escort (left) to combat the growing U.S. submarine threat. Using mass production techniques on a simplified design, a *kaikoban* could be produced in 90 days. By 1945, a typical ship carried sonar gear, one 4.7-inch gun, Type 22 radar on the foremast, and 120 depth charges, deliverable either by the stern rack or on one of the 12 depth charge throwers.

The Type 95 was the regular issue Japanese depth charge until 1943. Seventeen inches across and 30 inches long, its cylinder contained 242 pounds of explosive. The firing mechanism could be set to detonate at 100, 200, and 300 feet.

The Type 2 depth charge had similar dimensions to its predecessor, the Type 95, but it carried a larger (357 lbs.) explosive charge. Its firing mechanism could be set for detonation at depths of 100, 200, 300, 400, or 500 feet.

50 feet
Serious Damage

25 feet
Lethal Zone

January 1944

January 1944 saw Allied advances across the Pacific. MacArthur's forces invaded New Britain and continued to move up the coast of New Guinea. In the central Pacific U.S. forces consolidated the Gilbert Islands and prepared to attack the Marshalls. This drive across the atolls created new roles for U.S. submarines. They now scouted for the fleet, took periscope photos of potential landing beaches, acted as lifeguards for downed U.S. fliers, and interdicted enemy warships. However, the submarines continued to have their greatest impact on the Japanese merchant marine.

By January 1944 American submarine strength in the Pacific reached 100 boats, with 73 operating from Pearl Harbor and the rest from Australia. Submarines sank 335 merchantmen in 1943—more ships than Japanese construction yards could replace. Vital commodity imports for Japan's war industries declined by ten percent that year. Conditions were about to become much worse for the Japanese.

In 1943 U.S. codebreakers at Pearl Harbor deciphered Japan's merchant marine code. This allowed the U.S. Submarine Command to eavesdrop on the newly-formed Grand Escort Convoy system. U.S. subs consistently knew the destination, route, and speed of almost all Japanese convoys. The problem of locating the enemy in an immense ocean had been solved. The Americans organized groups of three to five subs into "wolf packs" and set out to attack Japan's convoy lifeline.

1943 Japanese Ship Losses	
January	25
February	11
March	26
April	22
May	33
June	27
July	21
August	20
September	39
October	30
November	49
December	32

Tambor's crew (top) rescues survivors after using its deck gun to sink a small Japanese freighter. On New Year's Day 1944, submarines *Herring*, *Puffer*, and *Ray* each destroyed a Japanese merchant ship. During the month of January, 45 American submarines made 113 attacks and sank a record 50+ Japanese ships.

New Guinea and the Solomon Islands January 1944

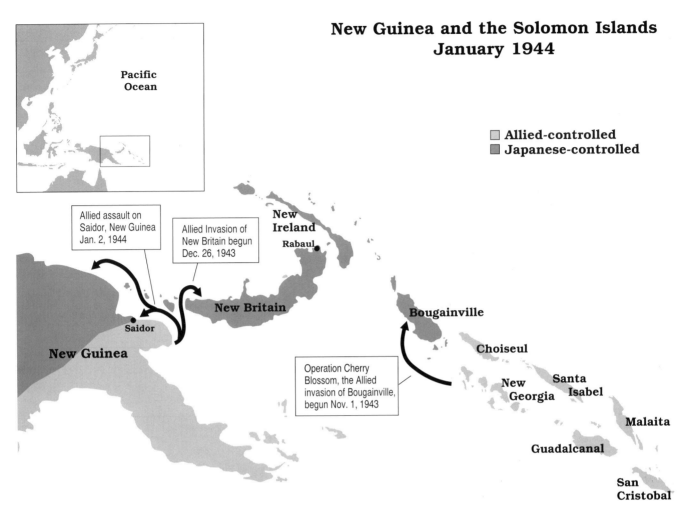

Pacific Ocean

☐ **Allied-controlled**
■ **Japanese-controlled**

Allied assault on Saidor, New Guinea Jan. 2, 1944

Allied Invasion of New Britain begun Dec. 26, 1943

New Ireland
Rabaul

New Britain

Saidor

New Guinea

Bougainville

Operation Cherry Blossom, the Allied invasion of Bougainville, begun Nov. 1, 1943

Choiseul

New Georgia **Santa Isabel**

Malaita

Guadalcanal

San Cristobal

A periscope photo (left) of a freighter torpedoed by *Aspro.* By January 1944, American and Australian forces had isolated the large Japanese base at Rabaul. This success brought them to the difficult job of clearing several major Japanese bases from the jungles of New Guinea's north coast. On January 2, 1944, having complete control of the air and sea as well as information from captured code books, General MacArthur's forces landed at Saidor, New Guinea, bypassing and cutting off two Imperial Army divisions. For the next six months, the Allies repeated this process along New Guinea's coast, never giving the undersupplied Japanese 18th Army time to regroup. U.S. submarines, operating from Brisbane, supported the invasion by attacking convoys which brought oil and supplies from Palau to Japan's large naval base at Truk. The submarines sank seven ships and the destroyer, *Sazanami* along this sea-lane in January.

Invasion of the Marshall Islands

The Allied victory in the Gilbert Islands accomplished two major goals: it reduced the Japanese threat to Australia's supply lines, and it brought the strategic Marshall Islands within range of American air power. Possession of the Marshalls would, in turn, bring Truk, Japan's main naval base in the South Pacific within range of U.S. land-based bombers.

Admiral Nimitz, informed by code breakers that the hard-pressed Japanese had written off the Marshalls, ordered U.S. forces to seize Kwajalein Atoll in the center of the chain by February 1, 1944. Code-named Operation Flintlock, the plan directed the 4th Marine Division to capture the northern island of Roi Namur, while the 7th U.S. Army Infantry Division took Kwajalein Island 44 miles to the south. At Admiral Spruance's request, the planners added Majuro Atoll, which could be converted to an excellent fleet anchorage.

Several days before the actual invasion, land-based U.S. bombers, staging from the Gilberts, attacked Japanese airfields in the Marshalls. In addition, 700 planes from 12 U.S. carriers bombed the bases. Operation Flintlock began

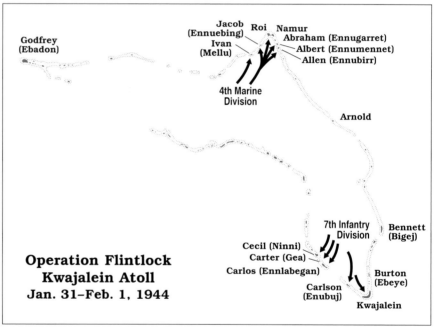

**Operation Flintlock
Kwajalein Atoll
Jan. 31–Feb. 1, 1944**

on January 31, 1944 with a tremendous air-sea bombardment of Kwajalein. The next day, Army and Marine divisions landed on the Atoll's two main islands. The 9,000 Japanese defenders fought with courage, but within a week the Americans secured Kwajalein Atoll at a cost of 8,680 Japanese and 332 U.S. lives. American forces took Majuro from its single Japanese caretaker on February 1st. The Atoll became a major fleet anchorage.

U.S. aircraft carriers (top) steam toward the Marshall Islands. Admiral Spruance assembled 375 ships of the U.S. Fifth Fleet for Operation Flintlock. The fleet's carrier force included 12 aircraft carriers with 700 planes, eight fast battleships, six cruisers, and 36 destroyers.

Kwajalein Atoll under attack (top opposite). Having learned important lessons from the costly Tarawa campaign, the U.S. Navy smothered Kwajalein Island with shells before the landing. Battleships, cruisers, and destroyers fired over 7, 000 14-inch, 8-inch, and 5-inch shells at the beaches.

Southern Pacific Ocean
Jan. 26–Feb. 1, 1944

U.S. submarines patrolled the Marshall and Caroline islands during Operation Flintlock. On January 26th, *Skipjack* sank the 6,666 ton seaplane tender, *Okitsu Maru*, and the fleet destroyer, *Suzukaze*, bringing troops to Eniwetok. Five days later, *Trigger* sank the large submarine tender, *Yasukuni Maru*, on its way to Truk. Finally, on February 1st, *Guardfish* sank the destroyer, *Umikaze*.

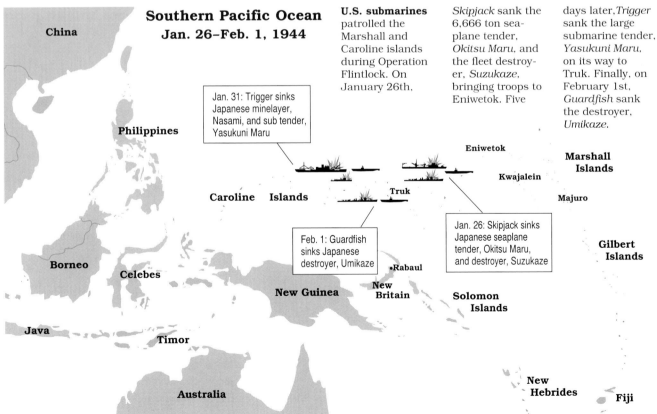

Jan. 31: Trigger sinks Japanese minelayer, Nasami, and sub tender, Yasukuni Maru

Feb. 1: Guardfish sinks Japanese destroyer, Umikaze

Jan. 26: Skipjack sinks Japanese seaplane tender, Okitsu Maru, and destroyer, Suzukaze

China

Philippines

Caroline Islands

Truk

Eniwetok

Kwajalein

Marshall Islands

Majuro

Borneo

Celebes

Java

Timor

New Guinea

New Britain

Rabaul

Solomon Islands

Gilbert Islands

Australia

New Hebrides

Fiji

Raid on Truk

The Americans' quick capture of Kwajalein allowed Admiral Nimitz the opportunity to attack Eniwetok ahead of schedule. The airfield at Eniwetok, the westernmost atoll of the Marshalls, was only 670 miles from the Truk Islands. Truk was the Imperial Navy's major base in the South Pacific. Its excellent anchorage sheltered the Combined Fleet, an important sub base, and several hundred aircraft on adjacent airfields.

To support the Eniwetok invasion, Admiral Nimitz ordered Operation Hailstone, a large carrier raid on Truk. Early on the morning of February 17, 1944 nine carriers from Task Force 58, escorted by six battleships, ten cruisers, and 28 destroyers, reached a point 90 miles east of Truk and launched the massive air raid.

Expecting attack, most of the Combined Fleet had evacuated Truk several days earlier. Nevertheless, American carrier planes found a few warships and over 40 merchantmen and naval auxiliary vessels still at anchor. U.S. fighters strafed the airfields while torpedo planes and bombers struck the ships. The raids continued for two days and destroyed 260 Japanese aircraft, three light cruisers, four destroyers, and 35 merchantmen at a cost of 29 U.S. aircraft. The attack ruined Truk as a major naval base and further isolated the large Japanese garrison at Rabaul, New Britain to the south.

Eniwetok fell to the U.S. Army and Marine invasion force on February 22nd after five days of hard fighting. Three hundred thirty-nine U.S. troops died in the battle. Only 66 of the 3,500 Japanese defenders survived. Truk, bypassed by the American ground forces, surrendered on September 2, 1945.

A U.S. aerial torpedo hits the 7,600 ton freighter *Amagisan Maru* (above) during the Truk air raid. The ship sank and carried its cargo of Zero fighter parts and vehicles to the bottom. U.S. planes also destroyed the large sub tenders, *Heian Maru* and *Rio de Janeiro Maru*, ending Truk's role as Japanese 6th Submarine Fleet headquarters.

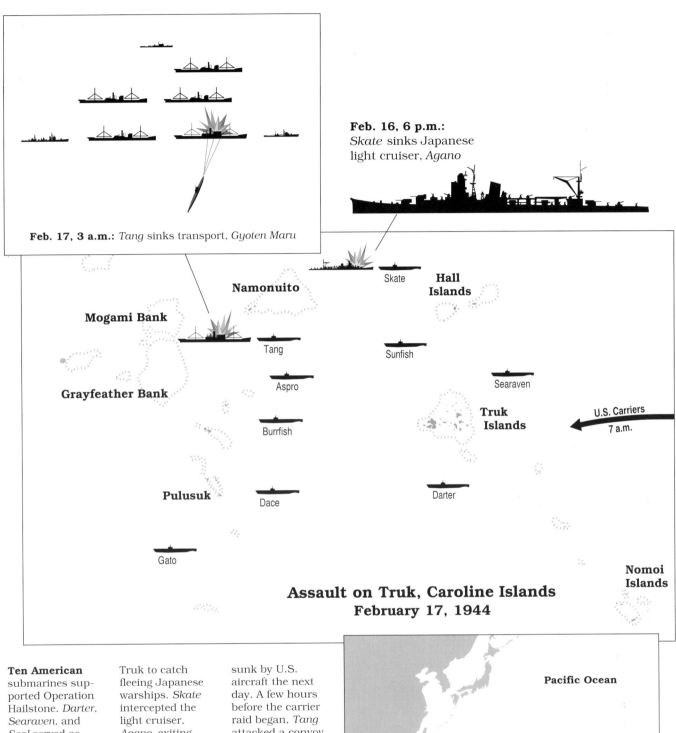

Feb. 17, 3 a.m.: *Tang* sinks transport, *Gyoten Maru*

Feb. 16, 6 p.m.:
Skate sinks Japanese
light cruiser, *Agano*

Skate

Hall
Islands

Namonuito

Mogami Bank

Tang

Sunfish

Aspro

Searaven

Grayfeather Bank

Truk
Islands

U.S. Carriers
7 a.m.

Burrfish

Pulusuk

Dace

Darter

Gato

Assault on Truk, Caroline Islands
February 17, 1944

Nomoi
Islands

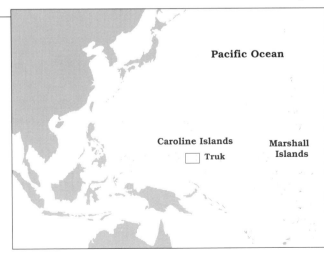

Pacific Ocean

Caroline Islands

Truk

Marshall
Islands

Ten American submarines supported Operation Hailstone. *Darter*, *Searaven*, and *Seal* served as lifeguards to rescue any downed U.S. pilots. The other seven submarines—*Skate*, *Tang*, *Aspro*, *Burrfish*, *Dace*, *Gato*, and *Sunfish*—patrolled in an arc around Truk to catch fleeing Japanese warships. *Skate* intercepted the light cruiser, *Agano*, exiting Truk's North Pass on February 16th and sank it with three torpedoes. One of the destroyer escorts, *Oite*, picked up several hundred *Agano* survivors and returned to Truk only to be sunk by U.S. aircraft the next day. A few hours before the carrier raid began, *Tang* attacked a convoy of five merchant ships. Three torpedoes hit the 6,800 ton freighter, *Gyoten Maru*, and the big ship quickly sank, taking down 1,000 troops of the 52nd Imperial Army Division.

93

Lifeguard Duty

In the autumn of 1943 the new Essex and Independence class aircraft carriers began to reinforce the U.S. Pacific Fleet. Admiral Nimitz organized these powerful ships into a group of task forces to conduct hit-and-run raids on Japanese outposts in preparation for the Gilbert Islands invasion. Expecting losses, Task Force Commander Pownall asked Admiral Lockwood if submarines could be stationed off the various target islands to rescue downed airmen. Lockwood readily assented, and formal submarine lifeguard patrols began on September 1st.

A month later on October 7, 1943 USS *Skate*, dodging Japanese bombs and artillery shells, rescued six airmen off Wake Island—the first successful lifeguard mission. During Operation Desecrate, the March 30, 1944 raid on Palau, USS *Gar* saved

eight aviators—a record that would last only a month.

On April 30th *Tang* waited as a lifeguard off Truk Atoll during the second major U.S carrier raid on that base. *Tang* rescued three airmen in the morning. A short time later, while searching for another flier, the submarine fought a gun battle with Japanese artillery on Truk before being forced to submerge. Wary of enemy shells, *Tang* requested fighter support, and under air cover, pulled another 19 pilots out of the water. *Tang* rescued 22 of the 32 fliers shot down on this raid. This feat so impressed Carrier Commander Marc Mitscher that he organized a special combat air patrol to protect submarines during rescues. The air patrol helped locate downed fliers, defend surfaced submarines, and guide ditching aircraft to the sub's vicinity.

Tang rescues
U.S. pilots (above) during the April 1944 carrier strike on Truk. A Kingfisher float plane from the battleship *North Carolina* helped *Tang* pick up the largest group of nine airmen. The plane landed on the water and towed three rafts bearing the downed fliers toward the sub.

Tang's skipper,
Richard O'Kane (top opposite) shown with the 22 U.S. airmen rescued off Truk in April 1944. *Tang* sank five merchantmen, including a loaded troopship, on its first patrol and now on its second set a record for greatest number of airmen rescued by a submarine in a single mission.

In addition to rescuing carrier pilots, U.S. submarines also served as lifeguards for B-29 squadrons raiding Japan in late 1944 and 1945. Subs picked up seven airmen in 1943, 117 in 1944, and 380 in 1945. Altogether, the silent service saved 504 U.S. airmen from capture or drowning during World War II.

Submarine Search Patterns

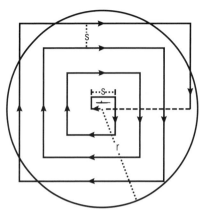

U.S. search patterns for locating survivors adrift on rafts. When the approximate ditching position was known, the search followed an expanding square course around the center of the suspected location. When the ditching site was not known, the search area was elongated, and rescuers used a parallel track approach.

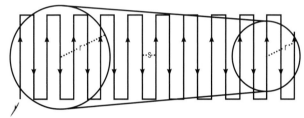

s = sweep spacing   r = search radius

Submarine Rescues of Allied Airmen

# of Airmen Rescued	Submarine	# of Airmen Rescued	Submarine
1	Archerfish; Argonaut II; Bang; Hackleback; Haddock; Hammerhead; Harder; Jack; Kraken; Plunger; Quillback; Rock; Saury; Sea Dog; Sealion II; Snook; Spikefish; Steelhead; Tilefish; Trigger; Trutta	5	Jallao; Plaice; Razorback; Stingray
		6	Aspro; Blackfish; Cabrilla; Icefish; Sea Owl; Skate
		7	Balao; Cobia; Grouper; Pomfret; Spearfish
		8	Gar; Sterlet
2	Bonefish; Charr; Guardfish; Hardhead; Perch; Sawfish; Sea Robin; Seawolf; Shark II; Silversides; Tench	9	Bluefish; Pipefish; Springer; Toro
		10	Pogy; Ronquil; Tinosa; Trepang
		11	Sea Fox
		12	Peto; Pintado; Sailfish; Scabbardfish
		13	Gato; Queenfish
3	Batfish; Bowfin; Bullhead; Cero; Chub; Searaven; Sturgeon; Tunny	15	Sea Devil; Whale
		16	Mingo
		17	Gabilan; Guavina
4	Bergall; Blueback; Kingfish; Threadfin	21	Ray
		22	Tang
5	Bream; Dragonet; Finback;	31	Tigrone

Japan's Vital Artery

Japan went to war for the oil in the Dutch East Indies. After the capture and rehabilitation of the oil fields, petroleum imports into the Empire rose from 300,000 barrels per month in January 1942 to 1.5 million barrels in June 1943. One hundred twenty-five ships transported oil between the Indies and the home islands.

In the first 18 months after the attack on Pearl Harbor, the Japanese lost only nine tankers to U.S. submarine torpedoes. The U.S. Navy did not have enough subs to effectively patrol all the merchant ship routes, and moreover, needed to use many of its boats in the South Pacific and Aleutian combat theaters. Defective torpedoes and the U.S. Command's failure to concentrate available subs across the main oil sea-lane that ran from Singapore to Japan further hampered the submarines' success.

This situation changed in the summer of 1943 when Admiral Lockwood made tankers a high priority target for his rapidly growing force. U.S. submarines sank 14 oil tankers in the last four months of 1943 and destroyed eight more in January 1944.

On February 19, 1944, two days after U.S. carrier planes bombed five tankers in the air raid on Truk, the submarine *Jack* detected a convoy of five tankers and three escorts northeast of Singapore. In a series of attacks from 4:42 a.m. until 10:33 p.m., the sub torpedoed four of the five oil tankers and one of the small escorts.

Mounting losses like these forced the Imperial Navy to adopt the inefficient defensive measure of shipping oil in slow convoys that hugged the coastline during the day and anchored in harbors at night. By the summer of 1944 this expedient reduced the flow of petroleum into Japan by 40 percent.

Lt. Comdr. Thomas Dykers USS *Jack*

The Navy commissioned USS *Jack* on January 6, 1943 and gave command to Lt. Comdr. Thomas M. Dykers. He took the submarine on its first war patrol off Japan's east coast in June 1943. *Jack* sank three ships on this initial voyage, then ran afoul of a patrol plane and took a close depth charge that blew the ship's stern out of the water and damaged an engine. On its third patrol *Jack* sank four tankers in one day—a record.

By the end of the war, the submarine had torpedoed nine cargo ships, five tankers, and a minesweeper.

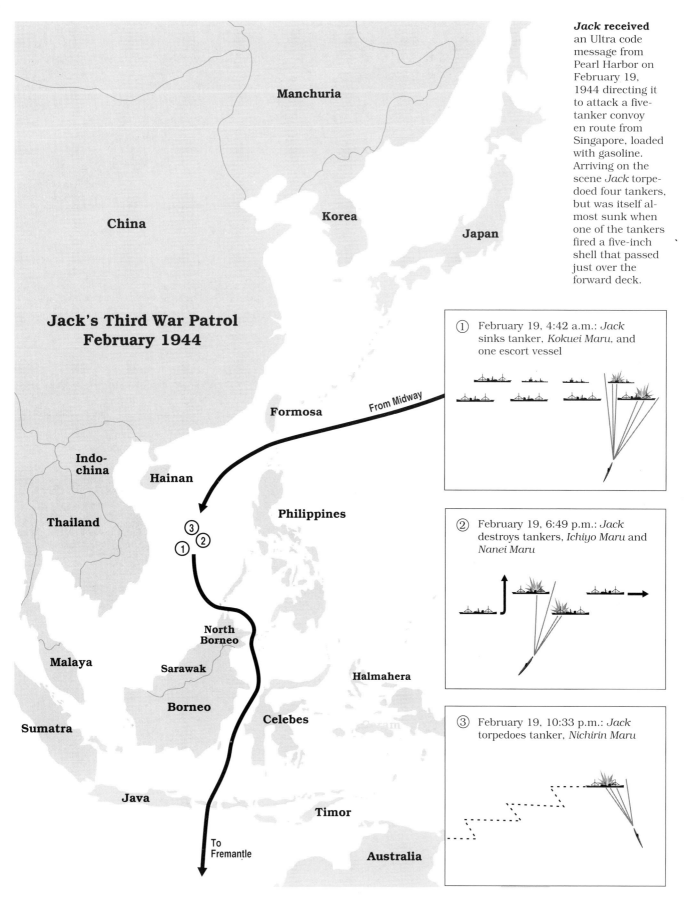

Jack's Third War Patrol February 1944

Manchuria

China

Korea

Japan

Formosa

From Midway

Jack received an Ultra code message from Pearl Harbor on February 19, 1944 directing it to attack a five-tanker convoy en route from Singapore, loaded with gasoline. Arriving on the scene *Jack* torpedoed four tankers, but was itself almost sunk when one of the tankers fired a five-inch shell that passed just over the forward deck.

Indo-china

Hainan

Philippines

Thailand

③ ②
①

North Borneo

Sarawak

Halmahera

Malaya

Borneo

Celebes

Sumatra

Java

Timor

To Fremantle

Australia

① February 19, 4:42 a.m.: *Jack* sinks tanker, *Kokuei Maru*, and one escort vessel

② February 19, 6:49 p.m.: *Jack* destroys tankers, *Ichiyo Maru* and *Nanei Maru*

③ February 19, 10:33 p.m.: *Jack* torpedoes tanker, *Nichirin Maru*

Bamboo Convoy No. 1

The seizure of the Marshall Islands in February 1944 and General MacArthur's continued advance in New Guinea threatened the Japanese Empire from two directions. In the central Pacific, if the Americans invaded the Marianas, bombers based on Saipan could reach Japan itself. To the south, the fall of New Guinea would allow the United States to retake the Philippines and cut the oil supply from the Dutch East Indies.

In Tokyo, General Tojo assumed dictatorial powers and ordered Japanese forces to hold to the death a new defensive line which ran through western New Guinea and the Marianas Islands. The Imperial General Staff reluctantly released two Army divisions based in China and sent them to New Guinea to stop MacArthur. The Japanese code-named the New Guinea reinforcement convoys "Bamboo" *(Take)*, and designated those headed for the Marianas as "Pine" *(Matsu)*.

Bamboo Convoy No. 1—nine Army transports crammed with troops and a small group of escorts—sailed from Shanghai on April 17, 1944. Rear Admiral Kajioka, whose forces had captured Wake Island early in the war, commanded the convoy from the minelayer, *Shirataka*.

Unaware that American code-breakers had deciphered his orders and alerted the U.S. submarine force, he took his ships down the Formosa Strait toward their first stop in Manila.

Nine days later on April 26th, submarine *Jack* intercepted the convoy off Luzon. Finding the many escorts alert on all sides, *Jack* fired two salvos of torpedoes into the convoy from long range. Most of them missed, but several struck the transport *Yoshida Maru No. 1*. It sank, taking an entire Japanese Army regiment with it. A shaken Admiral Kajioka put into Manila Harbor to regroup and pick up three more fleet destroyers for escort.

The voyage continued uneventfully until the morning of May 6th when *Gurnard* sighted the convoy's smoke. Lt. Comdr. Herb Andrews submerged the submarine and set an intercept course across the smooth, flat sea. On reaching position four hours later, he fired six torpedoes at two transports in the nearest column. He heard six hits as an onrushing destroyer forced *Gurnard* down to receive the first of a hundred depth charges. In this memorable attack Andrews sank three transports: *Tenshinzan Maru, Taijima Maru,* and *Aden Maru.*

The convoy landed on the island of Halmahera and most of the surviving troops were marooned there. *Jack* and *Gurnard* had stopped two Japanese Army divisions from reaching the front, and contributed to MacArthur's victory in New Guinea.

Gurnard (below) began its career on September 18, 1942 under the command of Charles Herbert Andrews. After one patrol in the North Atlantic, *Gurnard* moved to the Pacific. There, the submarine sank five ships and damaged several others before its notable attack on Bamboo Convoy No. 1 on May 6, 1944 during its fifth patrol. *Gurnard* ended the war with official credit for sinking ten Japanese merchant ships.

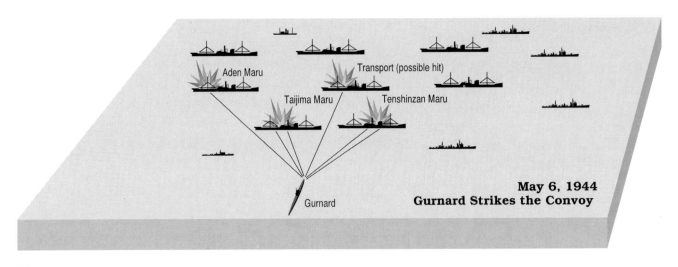

Aden Maru

Taijima Maru

Transport (possible hit)

Tenshinzan Maru

Gurnard

May 6, 1944
Gurnard Strikes the Convoy

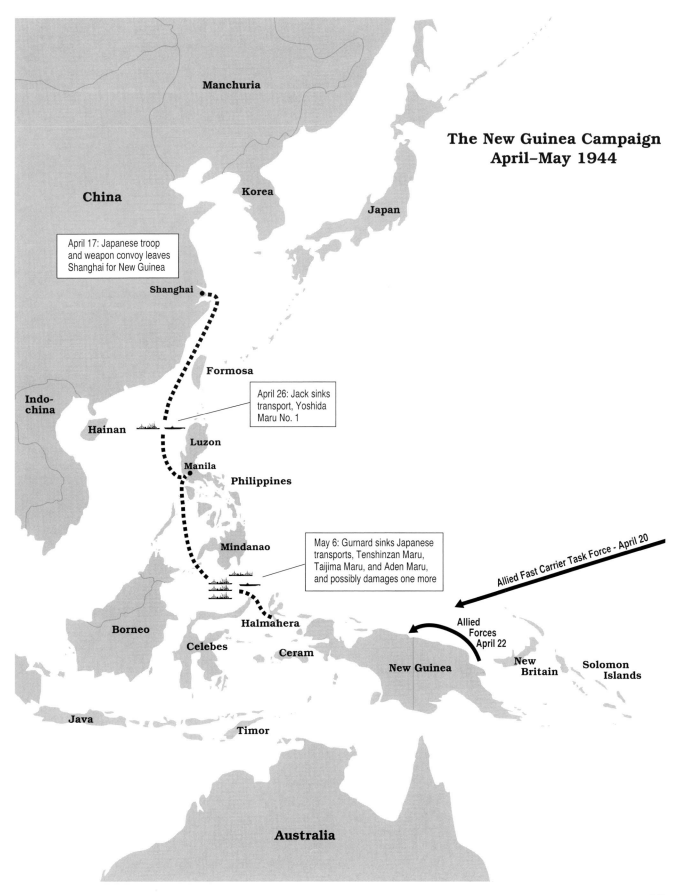

The New Guinea Campaign
April–May 1944

Manchuria

China

Korea

Japan

April 17: Japanese troop
and weapon convoy leaves
Shanghai for New Guinea

Shanghai

Formosa

Indo-
china

April 26: Jack sinks
transport, Yoshida
Maru No. 1

Hainan

Luzon

Manila

Philippines

Mindanao

May 6: Gurnard sinks Japanese
transports, Tenshinzan Maru,
Taijima Maru, and Aden Maru,
and possibly damages one more

Allied Fast Carrier Task Force - April 20

Borneo

Halmahera

Allied
Forces
April 22

Celebes

Ceram

New Guinea

New
Britain

Solomon
Islands

Java

Timor

Australia

Harder

On June 6, 1944, while Allied forces struggled desperately to hold the Normandy beachhead half a world away, the American submarine *Harder* approached Sibutu Passage, the seaway dividing North Borneo from the Philippine island of Tawi-Tawi. Commanded by Samuel Dealey, a soft-spoken Texan, *Harder* was on its fifth war patrol. Dealey and his veteran crew were making the third and final attempt to rescue six Australian coastwatchers. The Australians had monitored the Sibutu Passage for the last eight months and were exhausted by disease and constant pressure from Japanese patrols.

Harder approached the passage on the surface at 7:30 p.m. and detected a convoy of three tankers and two destroyers on its radar. Before the submarine could get into firing position, one of the

The Submarine Combat Insignia (above). A sailor had to pass difficult oral and written tests on every system of the submarine before he won his Dolphin Insignia. Once his boat completed a war patrol which sank one or more enemy vessels, he received the coveted Submarine Combat Pin.

destroyers spotted *Harder* in the moonlight and charged in to attack. Dealey calmly submerged, turned left, and when the range closed to 1,100 yards, put two fatal torpedoes into the onrushing destroyer, *Minatsuki*.

The next day around noon, *Harder* once again attempted to go through Sibutu Passage, this time at periscope depth. Another destroyer sighted the sub's periscope and attacked at high speed. With a zero bow angle, and at a distance of only 650 yards, *Harder* fired three torpedoes "down the throat," which sank the destroyer *Hayanami* in one minute. In the early dawn of June 9th *Harder* transited the passage and sent two small boats ashore to rescue the six Australians.

Sibutu Passage
June 6–9, 1944

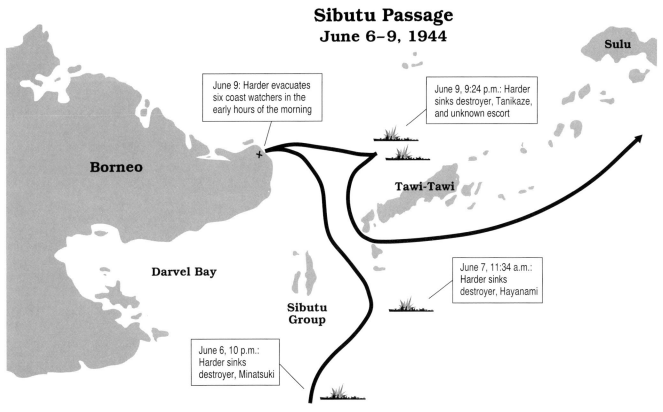

Sulu

June 9: Harder evacuates six coast watchers in the early hours of the morning

June 9, 9:24 p.m.: Harder sinks destroyer, Tanikaze, and unknown escort

Borneo

Tawi-Tawi

Darvel Bay

June 7, 11:34 a.m.: Harder sinks destroyer, Hayanami

Sibutu Group

June 6, 10 p.m.: Harder sinks destroyer, Minatsuki

Harder's Fifth War Patrol
May 26–June 21, 1944

Philippines

Mindanao

Borneo

Celebes

New Guinea

Java

• Darwin

Australia

From Fremantle

On May 4, 1944 Admiral Toyoda, ordered Operation A-GO into effect. This plan concentrated the Japanese Combined Fleet at Tawi-Tawi, a large anchorage off northeast Borneo, in order to block further advances by General Mac-Arthur's forces and to lure the U.S. Pacific Fleet into battle near the Palaus.

From this location Japanese shore-based aircraft could help their battered carrier forces in a fight with American carriers. *Harder*, after picking up the coastwatchers, ran into two escorts from Tawi-Tawi. The submarine fired four torpedoes and sank destroyer, *Tanikaze*, and an older patrol vessel.

Harder's **career** began on December 2, 1942 under Lt. Comdr. Samuel Dealey. Over the course of six war patrols *Harder* (below) sank ten merchantmen, four destroyers, and three frigates to earn the title "Destroyer Killer."

Invasion of the Marianas

The rapid fall of the Marshall Islands in early 1944 allowed the U.S. Joint Chiefs of Staff to advance Operation Forager, the planned invasion of the Marianas, to June 15, 1944. Admiral Nimitz ordered three Marine and two Army divisions to capture the main islands of Saipan, Tinian, and the former U.S. possession, Guam. The Navy believed the invasion of the Marianas, only 1,270 miles from Tokyo, would force the Japanese Combined Fleet into a decisive battle. The Army Air Force wanted to base its new long-range B-29 bombers on Tinian and attack the Japanese mainland.

After the loss of the Gilbert Islands in November 1943, the Japanese began a desperate effort to reinforce the Marianas with a series of convoys they codenamed *Matsu* (Pine). The first major troop movement, Matsu No. 1, began on February 26, 1944 when the 29th Army Division left Japan aboard three transports. Three days later, southeast of Okinawa, *Trout* torpedoed and sank one of the ships, the 9,400 ton *Sakito Maru.* Fourteen hundred soldiers of the 18th Regiment went down with the transport. The destroyer escorts depth-charged and sank *Trout* in the counterattack.

Matsu No. 2 left Yokohama on March 12, 1944 and ran into the U.S. submarine *Sandlance* the following day. *Sandlance* sank the transport, *Kokuyo Maru,* which carried 1,029 troops, and the light cruiser, *Tatsuta.* USS *Seahorse* attacked Matsu No. 3 near the Marianas on April 8th and sank two transports with 1,500 Japanese soldiers aboard. Matsu No. 4 successfully evaded American submarines, but Matsu No. 5, transporting a Japanese army regiment, lost two transports to the submarine *Silversides* on May

A Japanese bomber (above) shot down over the U.S. escort carrier, *Kitkun Bay,* during the invasion of the Marianas Islands. Operation Forager required the greatest logistical build-up the U.S. Navy ever mounted to supply the fuel, food, ammunition, and other military equipment for the invasion force of 127,000 troops.

10th. Attacks by *Shark* and *Pintado* in early June destroyed five of seven troop transports in Matsu No. 6, the last convoy.

Between January and June of 1944, U.S. submarines torpedoed 11 ships which carried 12,000 Japanese soldiers to the Marianas. Approximately 3,600 soldiers went down with the vessels and most of the survivors lost their equipment and unit cohesion. Although it cost two U.S. submarines, *Trout* and *Gudgeon,* the Japanese lost the equivalent of a division to the American submarine blockade.

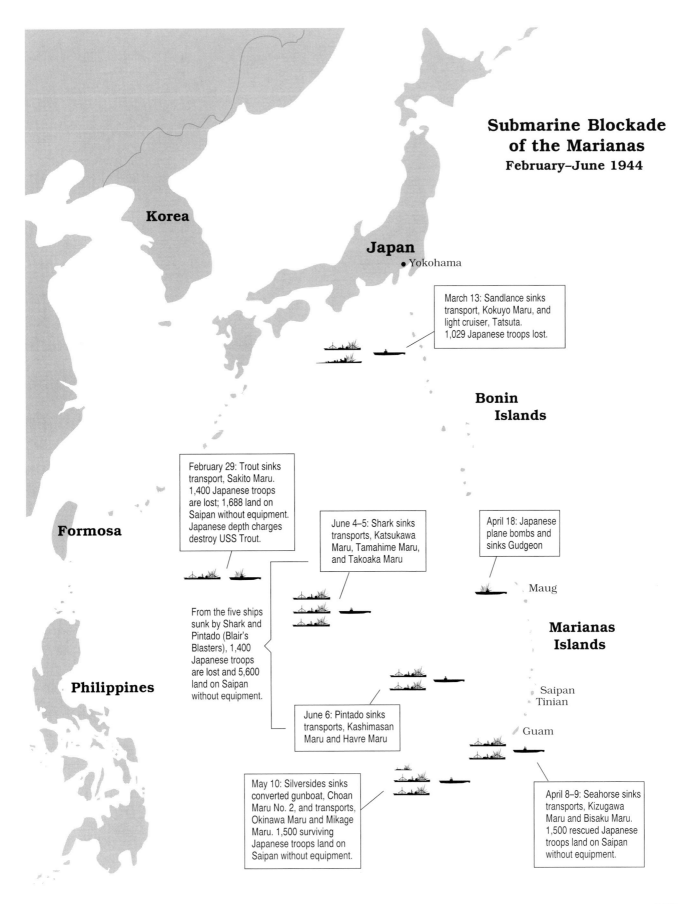

**Submarine Blockade
of the Marianas**
February–June 1944

Korea

Japan
• Yokohama

March 13: Sandlance sinks
transport, Kokuyo Maru, and
light cruiser, Tatsuta.
1,029 Japanese troops lost.

Bonin
Islands

February 29: Trout sinks
transport, Sakito Maru.
1,400 Japanese troops
are lost; 1,688 land on
Saipan without equipment.
Japanese depth charges
destroy USS Trout.

June 4–5: Shark sinks
transports, Katsukawa
Maru, Tamahime Maru,
and Takoaka Maru

April 18: Japanese
plane bombs and
sinks Gudgeon

Formosa

Maug

Marianas
Islands

From the five ships
sunk by Shark and
Pintado (Blair's
Blasters), 1,400
Japanese troops
are lost and 5,600
land on Saipan
without equipment.

Philippines

Saipan
Tinian

June 6: Pintado sinks
transports, Kashimasan
Maru and Havre Maru

Guam

May 10: Silversides sinks
converted gunboat, Choan
Maru No. 2, and transports,
Okinawa Maru and Mikage
Maru. 1,500 surviving
Japanese troops land on
Saipan without equipment.

April 8–9: Seahorse sinks
transports, Kizugawa
Maru and Bisaku Maru.
1,500 rescued Japanese
troops land on Saipan
without equipment.

Battle of the Philippine Sea

The U.S. Navy expected the Japanese to fight a naval battle over the Marianas and was not disappointed. When Admiral Ozawa, Commander of the First Mobile (Carrier) Fleet, realized the Americans were about to invade Saipan, he launched Operation A-GO on June 13, 1944. This plan called for the Japanese to attack the U.S. Fleet with 430 carrier aircraft and 500 planes flown into Guam from nearby bases. Unknown to Admiral Ozawa, the regional commander of land-based aircraft dispersed the aircraft instead of concentrating them on Guam.

Between June 13th and 18th U.S. submarines *Redfin*, *Flying Fish*, *Seahorse*, and *Cavalla* sighted the Japanese Fleet on its way to the Marianas and transmitted warnings to Pearl Harbor. On the morning of June 19th the Japanese carriers launched four attack waves at the U.S. Fleet, just 250 miles away. The aircraft were hardly on their way at 8:10 a.m. when U.S. submarine, *Albacore* worked past the escorts and fired torpedoes at the newly-commissioned heavy carrier, *Taiho*. A passing dive-bomber heroically crashed his plane into one of the torpedoes, but a second torpedo hit the carrier. Four hours later, *Cavalla* also intercepted the Japanese Fleet and sank the carrier, *Shokaku*, a veteran of the Pearl Harbor attack. Within a few minutes of each other that afternoon, both carriers blew up and went down with heavy loss of life.

The Japanese pilots threw themselves against the U.S. Fleet's reinforced combat air patrols and anti-aircraft fire, but only damaged a handful of U.S. ships. Three hundred-thirty Japanese planes were shot down. The next day the Imperial Navy's surviving ships retreated, conceding the victory and the Marianas to the Americans.

Albacore vs. Taiho

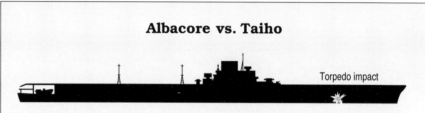

Torpedo impact

At 8:16 a.m. on June 19, 1944, Lt. Comdr. James Blanchard raised *Albacore's* periscope and saw the new 33,000 ton Japanese aircraft carrier, *Taiho*, approaching at 27 knots. The ship was launching 42 planes to attack the U.S. Fleet 250 miles away. Blanchard moved his submarine closer to the warship's track and at 9:09 a.m. fired six torpedoes at *Taiho*. Destroyers closed in and forced *Albacore* deep. Within minutes one of the torpedoes hit on the carrier's starboard side near the gasoline tanks. The explosion jammed the forward elevator and released gasoline fumes, but did not seriously harm the ship. An inexperienced damage control officer opened the carrier's ventilation system to clear the fumes and instead spread them throughout the vessel. At 3:30 p.m. *Taiho* blew up and sank into the 15,000-foot-deep Philippine Sea.

USS *Cavalla* (top opposite), was commissioned on February 20, 1944 and put under the command of Herman Kossler. On its first war patrol, in the Battle of the Philippine Sea, *Cavalla* torpedoed and sank the aircraft carrier, *Shokaku.*

Shokaku (above) began its career in the Pearl Harbor attack. The carrier's aircraft also helped take Wake Island and conquer the Dutch East Indies. During 1942 *Shokaku* fought in the Coral Sea and the Solomon Islands.

When the Americans landed on Saipan on June 15, 1944, Admiral Ozawa ordered the Combined Fleet's nine carriers and 46 escorting warships to "attack the enemy in the Marianas area." The approaching Japanese located

the U.S. Fleet on the evening of June 18th and prepared to attack the next morning. At 8:30 a.m. on June 19th the Japanese began to launch 370 planes from their carriers toward the American task

forces. U.S. submarines *Albacore* and *Cavalla* marred the take-offs when they torpedoed the carriers *Taiho* and *Shokaku.* The poorly coordinated air strikes ran into 300 U.S.

fighters and were slaughtered. Counting carrier and land-based planes, the Japanese lost 330 aircraft that day. The Americans lost 29 planes. This lopsided battle became known as the "Great Marianas Turkey Shoot."

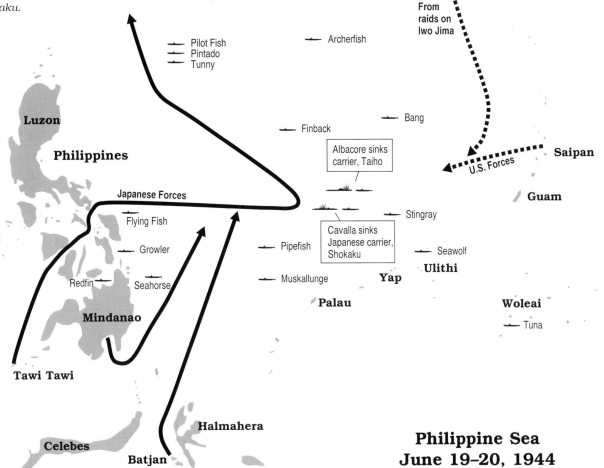

**Philippine Sea
June 19–20, 1944**

Convoy College

The loss of the Marianas had two serious naval consequences for the Japanese: it compressed their vital convoy routes into the South and East China seas, and it brought the large U.S. submarine force to Saipan, just 1,500 miles from these sea-lanes. Noting that many of the shipping lanes passed through the natural bottleneck south of Formosa, the U.S. Submarine Command designated the area "Convoy College."

Admiral Lockwood sent a series of wolf packs—groups of three to five submarines—to sever the flow of raw materials, munitions, and troops that passed through the

"College." The first submarines arrived in late June, and thereafter in overlapping sequence, a new group showed up each week or two. The Japanese responded with larger convoys, more destroyers, land-based air cover from Formosa, and four escort carriers to provide local air patrols over the merchant ships. Soon, under the weight of the submarine attacks, Convoy College became a moving battleground of torpedoed and sinking ships, exploding depth charges, attacking aircraft, and miles of flotsam and wreckage.

On the night of August 18th off northwestern Luzon, USS *Rasher*

detected Japanese convoy HI-71, southbound from Convoy College. *Rasher*'s commander, Henry G. Munson, counted 13 freighters and tankers, guarded by six escorts. He moved his ship in through a driving rainstorm, and at 9:22 p.m. torpedoed the 20,000 ton escort carrier, *Taiyo*, which blew up "with a column of flame a thousand feet high." The convoy split up, and over the next two hours *Rasher* torpedoed the 17,000 ton transport, *Teia Maru*, the 10,000 ton tanker, *Teiyo Maru*, and a small freighter, *Eishin Maru*. This patrol had the second highest tonnage sunk by a U.S. submarine during the war.

By the end of the summer, wolf packs from Pearl Harbor had sunk 56 ships in Convoy College, and submarines from Brisbane, such as *Rasher*, had added many more.

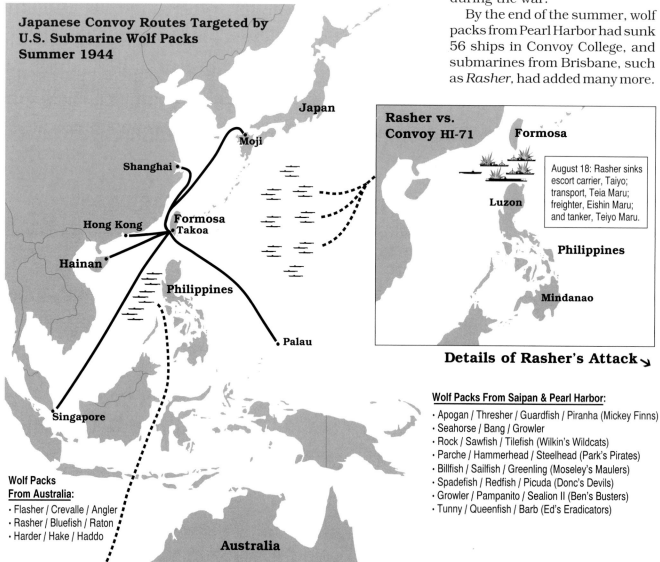

Japanese Convoy Routes Targeted by U.S. Submarine Wolf Packs Summer 1944

Japan

Moji

Shanghai

Hong Kong

Formosa
Takoa

Hainan

Philippines

Singapore

Palau

Australia

Rasher vs. Convoy HI-71

Formosa

Luzon

August 18: Rasher sinks escort carrier, Taiyo; transport, Teia Maru; freighter, Eishin Maru; and tanker, Teiyo Maru.

Philippines

Mindanao

Details of Rasher's Attack ↘

Wolf Packs From Saipan & Pearl Harbor:
- Apogan / Thresher / Guardfish / Piranha (Mickey Finns)
- Seahorse / Bang / Growler
- Rock / Sawfish / Tilefish (Wilkin's Wildcats)
- Parche / Hammerhead / Steelhead (Park's Pirates)
- Billfish / Sailfish / Greenling (Moseley's Maulers)
- Spadefish / Redfish / Picuda (Donc's Devils)
- Growler / Pampanito / Sealion II (Ben's Busters)
- Tunny / Queenfish / Barb (Ed's Eradicators)

Wolf Packs From Australia:
- Flasher / Crevalle / Angler
- Rasher / Bluefish / Raton
- Harder / Hake / Haddo

106

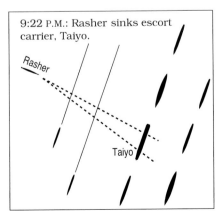

9:22 P.M.: Rasher sinks escort carrier, Taiyo.

Rasher

Taiyo

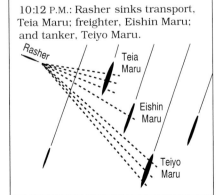

10:12 P.M.: Rasher sinks transport, Teia Maru; freighter, Eishin Maru; and tanker, Teiyo Maru.

Rasher

Teia Maru

Eishin Maru

Teiyo Maru

A lookout (above) scans night sky for Japanese planes. *Rasher* made its first war patrol from Fremantle in September 1943. The submarine, under the command of Edward S. Hutchinson, sank four merchantmen. Lt. Comdr. Willard Laughon took *Rasher* on its next three patrols, sinking two tankers and seven cargo vessels. Finally, veteran submarine captain, Henry Munson, commanded *Rasher* on its famous fifth patrol. *Rasher* received official credit for sinking 18 Japanese vessels during the war.

Loss of Harder

After *Harder's* incredible fifth war patrol, the boat arrived in Fremantle for rest and provisions. Although scheduled to return to the United States for leave and a new ship, Commander Sam Dealey persuaded Admiral Christie to let him take *Harder* out for one more patrol. He was ordered to lead *Haddo* and *Hake* in a wolf pack off the western Philippines.

Harder left Australia on August 5, 1944 and headed north. Two weeks later on August 21st, *Harder* joined *Haddo, Ray, Guitarro,* and *Raton* in a dawn attack on a large Japanese convoy in Paluan Bay. While *Harder* drew off the escort vessels, the other submarines sank four ships.

After surviving a severe depth-charging from the escorts, *Harder* and *Haddo* departed for their patrol area north of Manila. That night, August 22nd, near the infamous Bataan Peninsula, the two submarines attacked and sank three *kaikoban* frigates, *Hiburi, Sado,* and *Matsuwa.* These ships were survivors from convoy HI-71, ravaged by *Rasher* a few days before.

The next day, *Haddo* used its last torpedoes to sink the destroyer, *Asakaze,* and *Hake* joined the group. *Haddo* returned to New Guinea for a new batch of torpedoes, and *Harder* and *Hake* set course for Dasol Bay, just south of Lingayen Gulf. They arrived at dawn on August 24th and took station four miles offshore. Almost immediately, an old destroyer came out of the harbor on anti-submarine patrol. At 6:47 a.m. *Hake* spotted *Harder's* periscope 700 yards away. *Hake* decided to evade and at 7:28 a.m. heard a string of 15 depth charges. That night and for the next two weeks *Hake* tried to contact *Harder* without success. On September 10, 1944 *Hake* notified Fremantle that *Harder* was lost.

Comdr. Samuel Dealey USS *Harder*

Born in 1906 into a Texas first-generation family, Samuel Dealey graduated from the U.S. Naval Academy in 1930. After duty on the battleship USS *Nevada,* he went to submarine school in New London and then served aboard *S-24* in Hawaii. Sam Dealey assumed command of the *Harder* at its commissioning on December 2, 1942 and remained captain until its loss in August 1944. Admiral Thomas Kincaid wrote of Dealey: "He developed a superbly-trained submarine crew. He had faith in his officers and crew. His officers and men knew it and worshipped him." Congress awarded Samuel Dealey the Medal of Honor posthumously in 1945.

Fatal Depth-Charging of Harder

Patrol Boat 102

150 ft.

180 ft.

270 ft.

360 ft.

Harder

450 ft.

Fatal Shock Wave

Crush Depth 700 ft.

Water Depth 900 ft.

Patrol Boat 102
located *Harder* with its sonar and made five runs over the submarine, dropping six depth charges each time. The first group of six exploded at 150 feet. The next six were set to 180 feet. The third detonated at 270 feet, the fourth at 360 feet, and the fifth pattern exploded at 450 feet. After the last explosions, oil, wood, cork, and other debris rose to the surface.

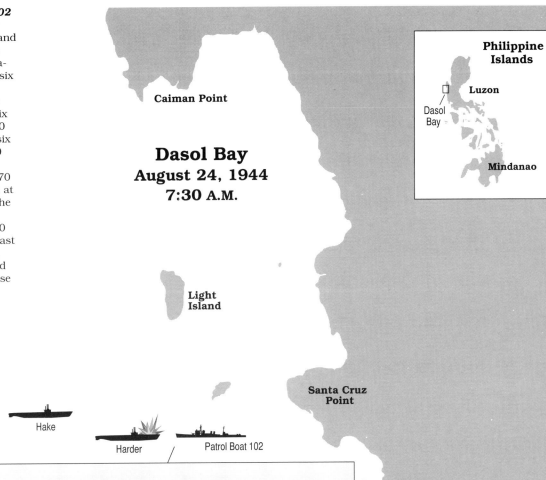

Caiman Point

Dasol Bay
August 24, 1944
7:30 A.M.

Light Island

Santa Cruz Point

Hake

Harder

Patrol Boat 102

Philippine Islands

Luzon

Dasol Bay

Mindanao

Patrol Boat 102

USS *Stewart* (DD 224), a Clemson class destroyer, began its career on September 15, 1920. Based in the Philippines in December 1941, the 1,200 ton warship was one of 13 destroyers attached to the U.S. Asiatic Fleet. All 13 destroyers took part in the defense of the Dutch East Indies, and *Stewart* suffered shell damage in action on February 18, 1942. Careless workers at Surabaya, Java damaged *Stewart* in dry dock and the Navy scuttled the ship on March 2, 1942 to prevent its imminent capture by the Japanese. After the fall of Surabaya, however, the Imperial Navy repaired the ship and sent it to sea as *Patrol Boat No. 102*. Manned by a Japanese crew, it sailed out of Dasol Bay on the morning of August 24, 1944 and fatally attacked the submerged *Harder* with 15 depth charges.

River Kwai Survivors

In August 1944, two more wolf packs from Pearl Harbor sailed for Convoy College. *Barb, Tunny,* and *Queenfish* arrived on station on August 24th. *Growler, Pampanito,* and *Sealion II*, the second pack, reached the Luzon Strait on August 29th. Unknown to the submariners, a drama unfolding in Singapore, 1,500 miles to the south, would soon involve them in one of the most poignant stories of World War II.

In 1942 when the Japanese took Singapore, they imprisoned 130,000 British, Australian, and Indian troops in POW camps. In violation of the Geneva convention, the Japanese sent 60,000 captured soldiers north into the Thai-Burmese jungle to build a 265-mile-long rail line through nearly impassable mountain terrain. Working from construction camps in the mosquito-infested forest, near starvation, and without medical care, the soldiers suffered from malaria, cholera, and beriberi and died in massive numbers. In just two years, the brutal treatment and the lack of food and medicine killed 13,000 POWs and reduced the rest to human wraiths.

When the railway was completed in early 1944, the Japanese decided to transport 10,000 of the fittest survivors to Japan to work in the mines and war factories. At Singapore, on September 4, 1944, the Japanese loaded 1,500 British and 718 Australian POWs aboard two transports: *Rakuyo Maru* and *Kachidoki Maru.* The two ships joined two freighters, two tankers, a destroyer, and three frigates, and sailed for Japan.

Back at Pearl Harbor, code-breakers intercepted the convoy's position reports and notified U.S. submarines of its route and composition, unaware of the Allied POWs aboard. *Growler* opened the attack at 1:54 a.m. on September 12th with a down-the-throat (bow-to-bow) shot that sank the destroyer, *Shikinami.* Four hours later, *Sealion* sank a transport, a tanker, and torpedoed the freighter, *Rakuyo Maru.* The freighter listed and sank slowly over the course of a day, allowing much of the crew and about 900 POWs to abandon ship. The Japanese picked up their surviving nationals, but left the POWs to drown. *Pampanito* followed the convoy and at 10:40 p.m. that night sank a tanker and *Kachidoki Maru.* Another 600 POWs were left struggling in the water. Japanese rescue ships picked up most of them the following day.

Three days later, *Pampanito* and *Sealion* passed through the area of the original attack. About four in the afternoon, *Pampanito* discovered dozens of oil-encrusted men in the water. Assuming the survivors were Japanese, the submarine eased up to a group to take a prisoner. Shock replaced caution when the men began to shout in English. *Pampanito's* captain, Pete Summers, ordered: "Take them aboard." By dusk the ship had rescued 73 Allied POWs. *Pampanito* radioed to *Sealion,* which entered the area just before dark and saved 54 more men before heading back to Saipan.

Pampanito (below) during refit at Mare Island Navy Yard. After two unsuccessful patrols, *Pampanito* joined *Growler* and *Sealion II* to form the "Ben's Busters" wolf pack in the Luzon Strait in August 1944. There it sank its first two ships: *Kachidoki Maru* and *Zuiho Maru.*

Kachidoki Maru (right). The U.S. Navy chartered the freighter, *President Harrison,* in November 1941 to help evacuate naval personnel from China to the Philippines. When the war broke out, a Japanese cruiser captured the ship, which had been run aground. The Japanese repaired it and renamed it *Kachidoki Maru.*

Rakuyo Maru (right) was one of two large transports the Japanese used in September 1944 to move 2,218 Allied survivors of the infamous "River Kwai" railroad to Japan. Mitsubishi Industries built the 9,500 ton, 477-foot-long passenger-cargo vessel in 1921.

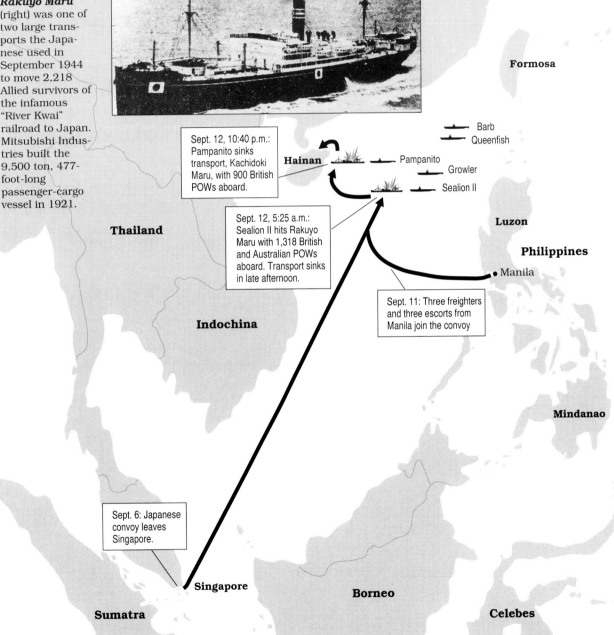

Formosa

Sept. 12, 10:40 p.m.: Pampanito sinks transport, Kachidoki Maru, with 900 British POWs aboard.

Hainan

Barb
Queenfish
Pampanito
Growler
Sealion II

Sept. 12, 5:25 a.m.: Sealion II hits Rakuyo Maru with 1,318 British and Australian POWs aboard. Transport sinks in late afternoon.

Luzon

Philippines

Manila

Sept. 11: Three freighters and three escorts from Manila join the convoy

Thailand

Indochina

Mindanao

Sept. 6: Japanese convoy leaves Singapore.

Singapore

Borneo

Sumatra

Celebes

South China Sea Convoy
September 1944

We Regret There Were No More

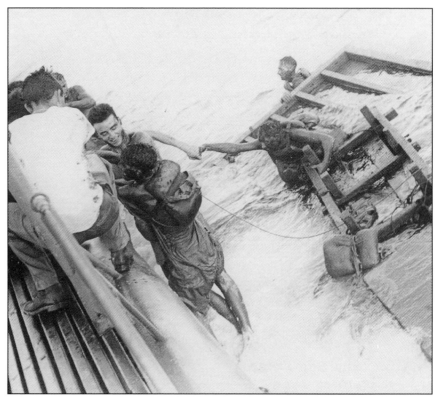

Then in a strange dream I fingered a rope that fell suddenly across my shoulders. In the dream I sat looking at it, wondering what it was. And then I heard shouts that came to me faintly through a mist of darkness. It disturbed me that this was a dream I did not understand. I put the rope over my head and felt myself being pulled backwards through the waves. There was a huge wall of steel, all shiny and wet, and I was dragged up it and splayed out on something firm and cold, something that didn't heave and dip. I could see a strange blur of faces; white faces with beards. And I could hear voices that were not Japanese. I realized, disinterestedly, that I wasn't, after all, going to die. A hand nudged under my neck and something trickled down my throat and exploded into fire in my chest. A deep drawling voice said softly, "Relax, fella. Everything's gonna be all right." I whispered, "Yanks," and fell into a wonderful unconsciousness.   —A.G. Allbury

The crews of *Pampanito* and *Sealion II* were horrified by the condition of the Allied POWs they brought aboard. Encrusted with oil, dehydrated, weak, and covered with sores, many could hardly grasp the rescue lines. Crewmen washed down the survivors and handed them below where the pharmacist's mate and his assistants gave morphine and cleaned the oil from their eyes, ears, and mouths. Volunteers fed the men small amounts of water while the cooks prepared tea, cocoa, soup, and toast for those capable of eating. Once the men were clean, the pharmacist's mate and his assistants treated their sores with sulfa powder and bandages. Then they wrapped the survivors in blankets and bunked them down in every available space.

At 1 a.m. on September 16th Pearl Harbor notified *Barb* and *Queenfish*—450 miles away—of *Pampanito's* discovery, and ordered the subs to assist with the rescue. The weather was turning stormy and conditions more precarious for the men in the water. The two submarines ran at full power until 9:10 p.m. when *Queenfish* picked up a convoy of 12 ships on radar. Two hours later, in one of the best single salvo shots of the war, *Barb* torpedoed and sank the escort carrier, *Unyo*, and the large tanker, *Azusa*.

Barb and *Queenfish* arrived at the rescue area early on September 17th and, fighting 20 knot winds, began their search. A little after 1 p.m. they located the first survivors. The men had now been in the water six days. Between them the two subs saved 32 Allied POWs. Winds increased to 60 knots the next day and ended the rescue effort. Altogether *Sealion*, *Pampanito*, *Barb*, and *Queenfish* saved 159 of the 1,318 British and Australians that sailed from Singapore aboard *Rakuyo Maru.*

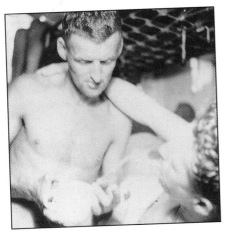

Sealion II responded to the urgent calls for assistance at full speed. Crewmen aboard the submarine (above) spotted their first survivors at 6:30 p.m. on September 15th.

The faces of POW survivors aboard *Pampanito* reflect their mistreatment in Japanese camps and their ordeal in the water.

Two oil-covered POWs (top opposite) rescued by *Pampanito* on the afternoon of September 15th. The men spent four days in the water.

Sealion II (left opposite) rescues survivors from *Rakuyo Maru* at dusk on September 15th. Many more POWs were in the water than the submarines could take aboard.

Seawolf's Last Run

In preparation for MacArthur's return to the Philippines, scheduled for October 20, 1944, guerrillas stepped up their harassment of Japanese forces in the Islands. U.S. submarines on "special mission" had been supplying the Philippine resistance with ammunition, food, medicines, and money since January 1943. By the fall of 1944 there were an estimated 65,000 organized insurgent troops throughout the country, a network of coast watchers, weather stations, and 120 small radio stations that passed intelligence to the Americans.

USS *Seawolf* was one of the subs that supplied the guerrillas. Now the boat returned to the Philippines for its 15th war patrol. Under Lt. Comdr. Albert Bontier, *Seawolf* sailed from Brisbane on September 21, 1944 for the new submarine base on Manus Island, north of New Guinea. There, the ship refueled and received orders to transport 17 U.S. Army special agents and their supplies to the east coast of Samar Island in the Philippines. *Seawolf's* planned route passed near U.S. forces invading Morotai Island. Casting off on September 29th, the submarine ran into unusual winds and tides which delayed its progress along the safety lane by 24 hours. U.S. surface forces knew American submarines used this designated lane, and it was therefore off limits to attack.

On October 3rd, the Japanese submarine, *RO-47*, attacked a U.S. task force supporting the Morotai invasion, and torpedoed and sank the destroyer-escort, USS *Shelton*. The Americans launched aircraft from the carrier, *Midway,* to help hunt down the Japanese submarine. One plane strayed into the safety lane and late in the morning mistook the surfaced *Seawolf* for the enemy boat. It dropped two bombs, which missed, and a dye marker on the diving submarine.

Eighteen miles away, the U.S. destroyer, *Richard M. Rowell,* received the sighting report from the plane and rushed to attack. At 1:10 p.m. the *Rowell* detected a

Seawolf (above) began its war career as part of the U.S. Asiatic Submarine Force based in Manila. Over the next three years and 14 war patrols, *Seawolf* sank at least 18 enemy ships and damaged many more. It conducted important photographic reconnaissance, and landed supplies to aid guerrillas in the Philippines.

submarine on its sonar. While the destroyer maneuvered to attack, *Seawolf* attempted to contact it on sonar by sending Morse code recognition signals.

Although he knew his destoyer was in the safety zone and it was extremely unusual for a submarine to signal, Captain Harry Barnard ordered an attack. He noted in his log: "1:16 p.m. Fired 24-charge hedgehog pattern at contact. Three explosions heard, two large boils [bubbles] observed off port beam, debris observed in the boils."

One of the great warships of the U.S. Navy was gone. *Seawolf* went down with all hands—82 crewmen and 17 Army special agents.

114

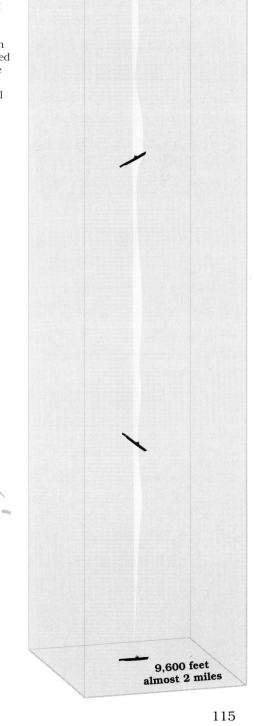

① Plane launched from U.S. aircraft carrier, *Midway*, drops two bombs (which miss) and a dye marker on *Seawolf*.

② USS *Richard M. Rowell* drops 24 hedgehogs on the submerged *Seawolf*. The submarine sinks with all hands.

U.S. sailors load a hedgehog depth bomb projector (above). The weapon fired a pattern of contact depth charges ahead of the destroyer which was almost impossible for a submarine to evade. Although the U.S. Submarine Command in Australia notified 7th Fleet Headquarters of *Seawolf*'s position, the information never reached the carrier, *Midway*, nor the destroyer, *Richard M. Rowell*, eager to revenge the torpedoed destroyer, *Shelton*. This communication breakdown led to the loss of the *Seawolf*.

Philippines

Samar

Oct. 3: U.S. destroyer, Richard M. Rowell, detects unidentified sub in the submarine safety land and drops hedgehogs, sinking Seawolf.

Seawolf refuels at Manus Island and picks up special agents destined for Samar, Philippines. Departs on Sept. 29.

Morotai

Manus

New Guinea

Australia

Seawolf's 15th War Patrol

From Brisbane Sept. 21, 1944

9,600 feet almost 2 miles

Battle of Leyte Gulf

After the fall of the Marianas, the Japanese expected the United States to invade the Philippines and prepared the SHO 1 operation to defend the islands. SHO 1 planned to use Japan's four remaining aircraft carriers—now almost empty of planes—as bait to lure the U.S. carriers away from their protective coverage of the invasion transports. With that accomplished, two powerful Japanese surface forces would converge on the invasion site and destroy the Allied ships.

When MacArthur's army landed at Leyte Gulf on October 20, 1944, the Japanese put the plan into effect. Admiral Kurita's First Strike Force of five battleships, 12 cruisers, and 17 destroyers sailed from Brunei on October 22nd, headed for Leyte Gulf. U.S.

submarines, *Darter* and *Dace*, spotted them the next night in Palawan Passage. At 5:24 a.m. *Darter* put four torpedoes into Admiral Kurita's flagship, the heavy cruiser, *Atago*. Although Kurita escaped, *Atago* went down in 30 minutes with 360 men. *Darter* also damaged the heavy cruiser, *Takao*. A few minutes later, *Dace* sank the heavy cruiser, *Maya*.

Alerted by the submarines, 259 U.S. carrier planes attacked Kurita's force the next day, sinking the super battleship, *Musashi*, and a destroyer. That night (October 24th) the Japanese Second Strike Force of two battleships, four cruisers, and 11 destroyers, ran into Admiral Oldendorf's battle line in Surigao Strait, just off Leyte. His six battleships (including five salvaged at

Pearl Harbor), eight cruisers, and 29 destroyers fought a wild running battle with the Japanese and sank two battleships, one heavy cruiser, and three destroyers.

Following Japanese expectations, at dawn on October 25th, the fast U.S. 3rd Fleet carriers under Admiral Halsey abandoned Leyte invasion forces to pursue Japan's carriers to the north. The surviving ships of Admiral Kurita's First Strike Force drove through San Bernardino Strait and made for the U.S. beachheads only to be stopped by several hundred U.S. escort carrier planes and a handful of outgunned U.S. destroyers. Their strong defense confused Admiral Kurita and he broke off the attack at noon and retreated northward, ensuring final Japanese defeat.

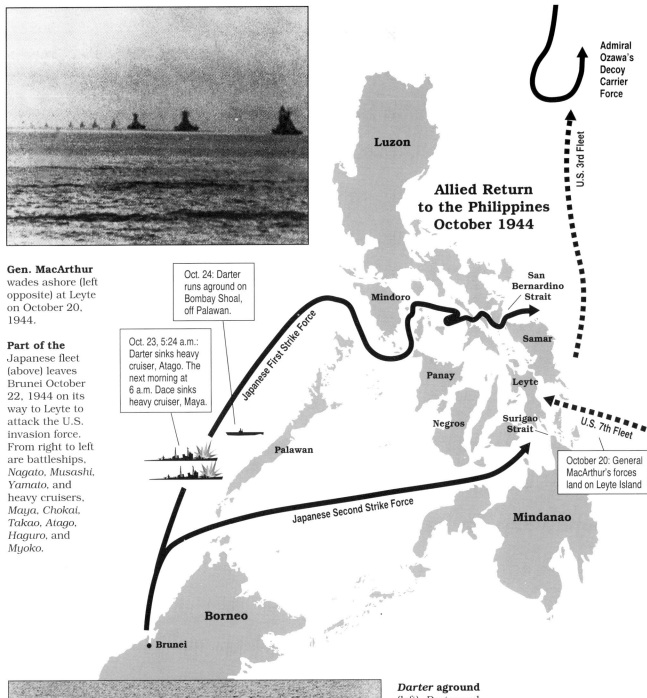

**Allied Return
to the Philippines
October 1944**

Gen. MacArthur wades ashore (left opposite) at Leyte on October 20, 1944.

Part of the Japanese fleet (above) leaves Brunei October 22, 1944 on its way to Leyte to attack the U.S. invasion force. From right to left are battleships, *Nagato, Musashi, Yamato,* and heavy cruisers, *Maya, Chokai, Takao, Atago, Haguro,* and *Myoko.*

Oct. 24: Darter runs aground on Bombay Shoal, off Palawan.

Oct. 23, 5:24 a.m.: Darter sinks heavy cruiser, Atago. The next morning at 6 a.m. Dace sinks heavy cruiser, Maya.

October 20: General MacArthur's forces land on Leyte Island

Admiral Ozawa's Decoy Carrier Force

U.S. 3rd Fleet

U.S. 7th Fleet

Japanese First Strike Force

Japanese Second Strike Force

Luzon

Mindoro

San Bernardino Strait

Samar

Panay

Leyte

Negros

Surigao Strait

Palawan

Mindanao

Borneo

Brunei

***Darter* aground** (left). *Darter* and *Dace* planned to finish off the damaged heavy cruiser, *Takao,* in a night attack. During a high-speed run to get ahead of the slowly-retreating *Takao, Darter* ran aground on the Bombay Reef. Unable to free itself, the crew set demolition charges, and transferred to the waiting *Dace.* USS *Nautilus* arrived on October 31st and finished the destruction of *Darter* with 55 six-inch shells.

117

Abandon Ship!

A few hours before Admiral Kurita struck the American escort carrier forces in Leyte Gulf on October 25, 1944, USS *Tang* fought its last battle in the Formosa Strait. Commanded by Richard O'Kane, the submarine patrolled the Formosa Strait to interdict Japanese reinforcements bound for the Philippine Islands.

On the night of October 24th, with five ships already to its credit on this fifth war patrol, *Tang* detected a large, heavily-escorted convoy hugging the China coast. In a daring surface attack, O'Kane sank several ships and damaged a transport. The submarine drew off a few miles to load its last two torpedoes before returning to finish off the damaged ship.

Tang closed the listing transport, and at 900 yards, fired the two torpedoes. The first went straight toward the target, but the last torpedo curved sharply to the left in a circular run and headed back toward the *Tang*. O'Kane shouted for emergency speed and put the rudder hard over to clear the torpedo's turning circle but 20 seconds later the Mark 18 electric torpedo hit the submarine's stern.

The tremendous explosion instantly flooded the three after compartments, killing the crewmen in them. Although *Tang's* stern plunged immediately to the bottom, 180 feet below, forward buoyancy kept 25 feet of the bow above the water and the submarine assumed a 40 degree angle between the seabed and the surface. Three of the nine officers and men on the bridge, including O'Kane, were thrown clear and managed to stay afloat in calm seas. It was small consolation to the men swimming in the water to watch *Tang's* first torpedo hit home and sink the transport. Forty-five survivors remained trapped inside the stricken submarine.

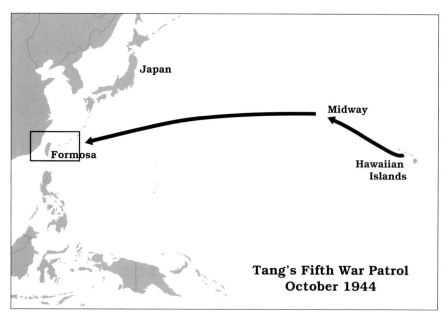

**Tang's Fifth War Patrol
October 1944**

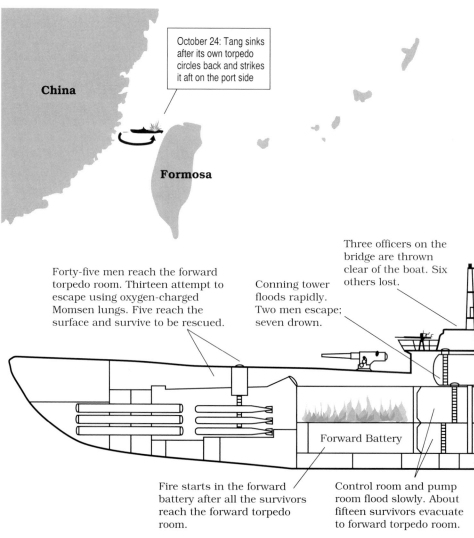

October 24: Tang sinks after its own torpedo circles back and strikes it aft on the port side

Forty-five men reach the forward torpedo room. Thirteen attempt to escape using oxygen-charged Momsen lungs. Five reach the surface and survive to be rescued.

Conning tower floods rapidly. Two men escape; seven drown.

Three officers on the bridge are thrown clear of the boat. Six others lost.

Forward Battery

Fire starts in the forward battery after all the survivors reach the forward torpedo room.

Control room and pump room flood slowly. About fifteen survivors evacuate to forward torpedo room.

USS Tang
Twenty Seconds After Torpedo Hit

180 ft.

The map (top opposite) shows *Tang's* route on its fifth war patrol. U.S. submarines *Darter*, *Shark II*, and *Tang* were all lost on October 24, 1944.

Aboard *Tang*
10 men survived in the sealed forward torpedo room which contained the escape trunk, 15 in the control room, and 20 more in the crew's quarters. A few minutes after the explosion, control room personnel decided to level off *Tang* on the bottom to protect the intact bow from Japanese attack and make going forward easier. They manually flooded the ballast tanks and settled the submarine on the sea floor at 180 foot depth. After burning classified documents, the 15 men in the slowly-flooding control room made their way to the forward torpedo compartment. A half hour later, the 20 survivors from the crew's quarters also reached the forward torpedo room. Forty-five survivors now gathered near the escape hatch. Smoke from a battery fire and carbon dioxide build-up made breathing difficult for the trapped men and sapped their will to survive. The escape equipment proved hard to operate and only five men reached the surface and stayed afloat long enough to be picked up by the Japanese the next morning. Altogether nine men, including Captain Richard O'Kane, survived to be taken prisoner by the Japanese. O'Kane was awarded the Medal of Honor after the war.

Fifteen Minutes After Torpedo Hit

After battery space partially floods. Twenty men escape to forward torpedo room.

Boat whips violently when the torpedo hits. After torpedo room, maneuvering room, after engine room, and all adjacent tanks flood rapidly. No survivors in the three after compartments.

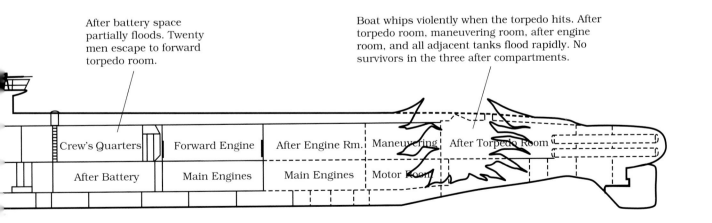

Crew's Quarters | Forward Engine | After Engine Rm. | Maneuvering | After Torpedo Room

After Battery | Main Engines | Main Engines | Motor Room

Torpedo Damage to USS Tang

The Biggest Carrier

On November 18, 1944 at a secret shipping yard in Tokyo Bay, the Japanese commissioned the super aircraft carrier, *Shinano*. Originally designed as a sister ship to the mighty battleships, *Yamato* and *Musashi*, *Shinano* displaced 72,000 tons fully loaded, sailed at 27 knots, and carried over 60 planes. The Imperial Navy, expecting daylight B-29 raids to begin over Tokyo at any time, decided to move *Shinano* to the protected Inland Sea to await the final battle—the Allied invasion of Japan.

Shinano's captain, Toshio Abe, decided to make a high-speed run to the Inland Sea, escorted by three destroyers. He expected darkness to mask his ship from prying aircraft and speed to help elude the numerous U.S. submarines off Tokyo Bay. At 6 p.m. on November 28th, *Shinano* hoisted anchor, headed out to sea at 20 knots, and began zig-zagging to confuse any nearby submarines. Two and half hours later, USS *Archerfish* detected

Shinano on SJ radar at a distance of 12 miles. Comdr. Joseph Enright chased the contact at full speed, but the carrier group moved slightly faster than *Archerfish*. It looked as if the *Shinano* would escape when at 3 a.m. the group zigged back toward the submarine. At 3:17 a.m. Enright fired six torpedoes at the carrier and scored four hits.

The torpedoes struck between the armor and the hull, and ripped four large holes in the ship. Water flooded through unfinished bulkheads, around loose cables and pipes, and through unsealed watertight doors. Capt. Abe refused to slow the carrier until the increasing list forced him to stop. There were not enough working pumps to handle the water, and just before 11 a.m. *Shinano* capsized and took down 1,435 officers and men.

Archerfish (below) was commissioned into the Navy on September 4, 1943 and had a relatively uneventful career until it sighted and sank *Shinano* on November 29, 1944.

Hokkaido

Honshu

Tokyo

Inland Sea

Shikoku

Kyushu

**Japan
November 29, 1944**

3:17 a.m.: Archerfish torpedoes Japanese carrier, Shinano.
10:55 a.m.: Shinano sinks.

Shinano's Torpedo Hits

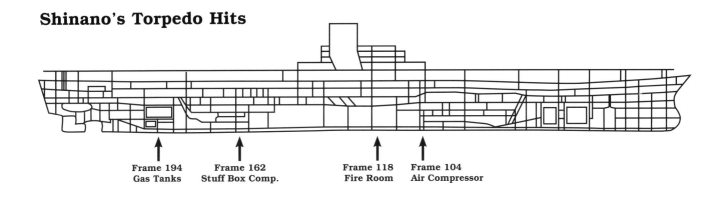

Frame 194
Gas Tanks

Frame 162
Stuff Box Comp.

Frame 118
Fire Room

Frame 104
Air Compressor

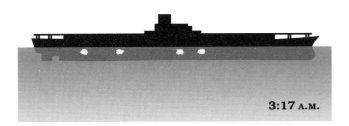

3:17 A.M.

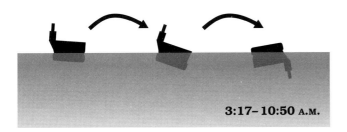

3:17– 10:50 A.M.

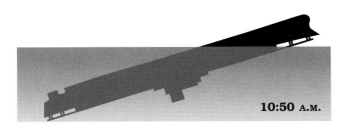

10:50 A.M.

10:55 A.M.

Archerfish Log

0317 Heard and observed first hit just inside stern near props and rudder. Large ball of fire climbed his side. Second hit heard and observed. This was about 50 yards forward of the first. With hits seen, a destroyer about 500 yards on our quarter. Started deep. Four more properly timed hits on our way down.

[First torpedo struck gas tanks near frame 194 aft. Within thirty seconds, three more torpedoes struck: at frames 162, 118, and 104. There were actually only four hits.]

0325 Breaking up noises started immediately. With the bright moonlight the identification is quite accurate. . . . Started receiving a total of 14 depth charges. Closest one was perhaps 300 yards away.

0345 Last depth charge. The hissing, sputtering, and breaking noises continued. At one time they covered 90 degrees of scale on the sound receiver.

0405 Last breaking up noise. Credit is claimed for a sinking because of these items: a) Six certain hits (two observed) b) Heavy screws stopped and did not restart c) Loud breaking up noises for 47 minutes d) Escorts gave us slight attention and closed carrier, probably picking up survivors.

0610 Daylight and first periscope observation. Nothing in sight.

[Archerfish had lost sight of Shinano at 0610. The ship actually sank at 1055.]

Flasher

The U.S. submarine war against Japan's merchant marine reached its crescendo in December 1944. Even heavily-escorted ships ran a high risk of destruction, as the fate of two tanker convoys demonstrated that month.

It was USS *Flasher's* fifth war patrol. On the morning of December 4th, while threading its way through rain squalls and a heavy swell, the submarine sighted an oncoming convoy 13 miles away and dived to intercept. A short time later, a Japanese destroyer loomed out of the mist at 2,000 yards and *Flasher* put two torpedoes into it. Spotting a large tanker beyond the listing destroyer, Commander George Grider fired four more torpedoes and scored two hits before another destroyer forced him deep.

After evading 16 close depth charges, *Flasher* reloaded its tubes and pressed in for another attack. The second Japanese destroyer, assuming the submarine was sunk or driven off, made the tactical mistake of stopping by the tanker. At 12:51 p.m. *Flasher* torpedoed this warship, and six hours later, finished off the burning and abandoned tanker.

The submarine continued to patrol off Indochina and on December 21st, just 12 miles off the coast, detected a convoy of five large tankers, protected by four escorts. Blocked by the patrol boats from a seaward approach, Grider decided to come in on the surface from the land side. At 4:46 a.m. *Flasher* torpedoed the first two ships in the column and just after "the second tanker blew up and illuminated the area like a night football game," Grider swung the submarine around and torpedoed and sank the third tanker. The tremendous explosions confused the escorts and *Flasher* made its escape on the surface without being sighted.

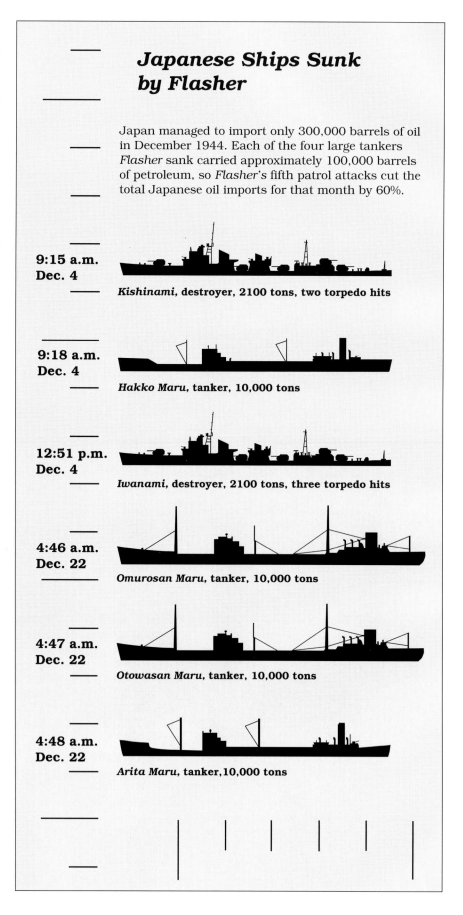

Japanese Ships Sunk by Flasher

Japan managed to import only 300,000 barrels of oil in December 1944. Each of the four large tankers *Flasher* sank carried approximately 100,000 barrels of petroleum, so *Flasher's* fifth patrol attacks cut the total Japanese oil imports for that month by 60%.

9:15 a.m. Dec. 4
Kishinami, destroyer, 2100 tons, two torpedo hits

9:18 a.m. Dec. 4
Hakko Maru, tanker, 10,000 tons

12:51 p.m. Dec. 4
Iwanami, destroyer, 2100 tons, three torpedo hits

4:46 a.m. Dec. 22
Omurosan Maru, tanker, 10,000 tons

4:47 a.m. Dec. 22
Otowasan Maru, tanker, 10,000 tons

4:48 a.m. Dec. 22
Arita Maru, tanker, 10,000 tons

Flasher's Fifth War Patrol
December 1944

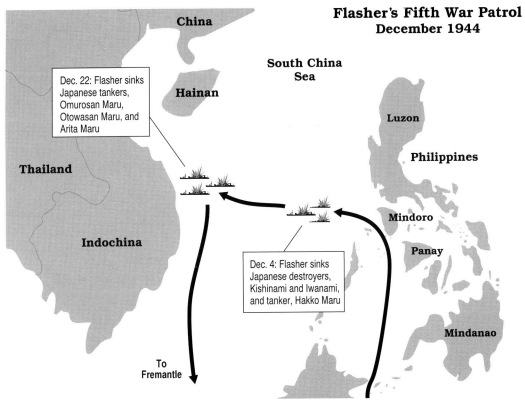

China

South China Sea

Hainan

Dec. 22: Flasher sinks Japanese tankers, Omurosan Maru, Otowasan Maru, and Arita Maru

Thailand

Luzon

Philippines

Indochina

Dec. 4: Flasher sinks Japanese destroyers, Kishinami and Iwanami, and tanker, Hakko Maru

Mindoro

Panay

Mindanao

To Fremantle

USS *Flasher* (below). Lt. Comdr. Reuben Whitaker took command of the newly commissioned *Flasher* on September 25, 1943. *Flasher* sank four ships on its first patrol and three more on the second. The submarine sank the light cruiser, *Oi*, and six more merchantmen on its third and fourth patrols. In November 1944, Whitaker turned over command to George Grider who had served aboard *Wahoo*. *Flasher* ended the war with the highest record for total Japanese tonnage sunk: 21 ships, comprising 100,231 tons.

January 1945

By the beginning of 1945 the American submarine campaign had choked off the imports Japan needed to continue the war. The destruction of over 600 Japanese merchant ships by U.S. submarines in 1944 caused imports of already scarce industrial commodities to decline by 40 percent. Oil stocks collapsed and the Japanese hid their few remaining warships in the Inland Sea. One hundred fifty-six U.S. submarines now operated in the Pacific, and during 1944 they had sunk—in addition to the merchant ships—seven aircraft carriers, one battleship, nine cruisers, and 30 destroyers. Fearful sailors on the Asian mainland told each other that a mariner could walk to Japan on American periscopes.

On January 8, 1945 General MacArthur's forces landed at Lingayen Gulf on the Philippines' main island of Luzon. American ships beat off severe kamikaze raids while U.S. carrier planes attacked Japanese air bases on Formosa and the Chinese mainland. The Japanese Army on Luzon retreated into the mountains and continued to fight until the end of the war.

By the end of January the gigantic U.S. Third Fleet was back at Ulithi Atoll to replenish its stores and prepare for the invasion of Iwo Jima, a small island halfway between the Marianas and Tokyo. Iwo was a major Japanese fighter base used to attack B-29s from Guam on their way to bomb Japan. With the island in American hands, U.S. fighters could escort B-29 superfortresses all the way to Tokyo, and damaged bombers could make emergency landings on the small island. On February 19, 1945 hundreds of Allied ships surrounded Iwo Jima and landed three U.S. Marine divisions into one of the bloodiest battles of the Pacific war.

U.S. Marines raise the flag at Iwo Jima (below). It took three U.S. Marine divisions a month to conquer the 21,000 Japanese defenders on the five-mile-long island. U.S. Marine casualties were 6,800 killed and 19,000 wounded. Only 216 Japanese survived.

U.S. carriers in camouflage at Ulithi Atoll in the western Caroline Islands (bottom). The U.S. Navy's construction battalions (Seebees) transformed Ulithi's 30 islets and its deep lagoon into the major forward supply base for the final year of the war.

124

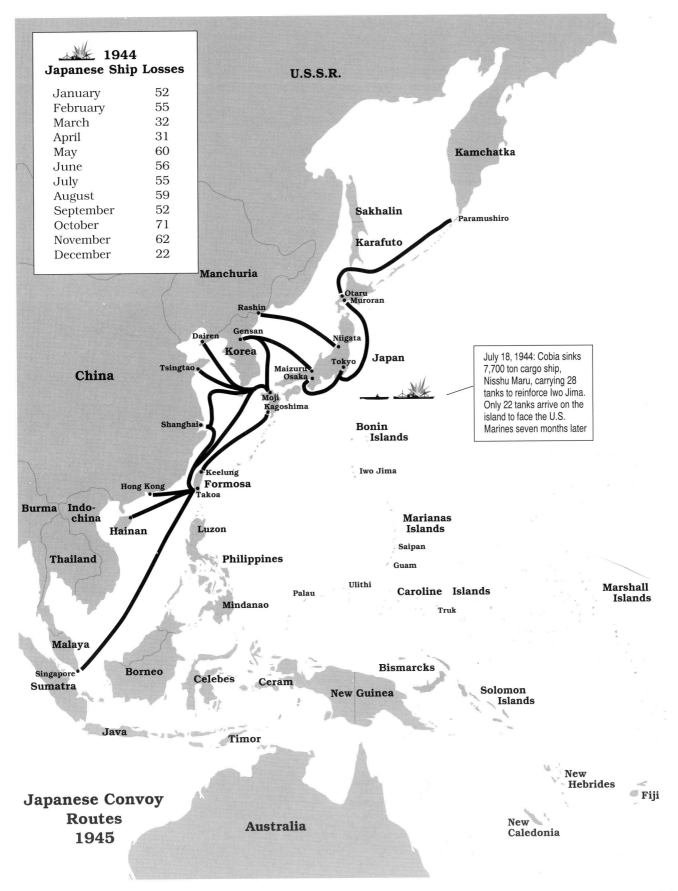

1944 Japanese Ship Losses

January	52
February	55
March	32
April	31
May	60
June	56
July	55
August	59
September	52
October	71
November	62
December	22

U.S.S.R.

Kamchatka

Paramushiro

Sakhalin

Karafuto

Manchuria

Otaru
Muroran

Rashin

Dairen
Gensan
Korea
Niigata

Tsingtao
Maizuru
Osaka
Tokyo
Japan

China

Moji
Kagoshima

Shanghai

July 18, 1944: Cobia sinks
7,700 ton cargo ship,
Nisshu Maru, carrying 28
tanks to reinforce Iwo Jima.
Only 22 tanks arrive on the
island to face the U.S.
Marines seven months later

Bonin
Islands

Iwo Jima

Keelung
Hong Kong
Formosa
Takoa

Burma Indo-
china

Hainan

Luzon

Philippines

Marianas
Islands

Saipan

Guam

Thailand

Palau

Ulithi
Caroline Islands

Truk

Marshall
Islands

Mindanao

Malaya

Borneo

Celebes
Ceram

Bismarcks

Solomon
Islands

Singapore
Sumatra

New Guinea

Java

Timor

New
Hebrides
Fiji

**Japanese Convoy
Routes
1945**

Australia

New
Caledonia

Into the Sea of Japan

The Japanese economy staggered along in the summer of 1945, sustained only by imports from Manchuria and Korea across the Sea of Japan. Mine fields barred the entrances into the Sea and no U.S. submarines had attempted passage since *Wahoo's* presumed loss to mines in October 1943.

The introduction of the new FM sonar, which allowed American submarines to detect mines while submerged, ended this sanctuary. After careful testing of the device, the Submarine Command at Pearl Harbor organized Operation Barney, a June invasion of the Sea of Japan, using nine U.S. submarines split into three wolf packs.

On May 29th the first wolf pack —*Spadefish, Crevalle* and *Sea Dog*— sailed from Guam, headed for Tsushima Strait, the southern entrance to the Sea. The next day, *Tunny, Bonefish* and *Skate* departed, and finally *Flying Fish, Tinosa,* and *Bowfin* left on their patrols. Their orders directed them to traverse 1,600 miles to the Strait, and on the morning of June 4th submerge at the entrance and creep under the mine fields in the passage.

Estimating the mines to be in four long rows moored at an average depth of 70 feet, the submarines went down below 120 feet to clear the fields. The FM sonar sets detected most of the mines, and only *Skate* and *Tinosa* had the terrifying experience of scraping a mine cable during the submerged run.

Once inside the Sea of Japan the three wolf packs proceeded to their stations and on June 9th began synchronized attacks. Covering northwest Honshu, *Spadefish, Crevalle* and *Sea Dog* sank 14 merchant ships over the course of the two week patrol. Farther to the south, *Skate* and *Bonefish* destroyed five cargo ships, and *Skate* torpedoed the Japanese submarine, *I-122.* Destroyers sank *Bonefish* on June 18th in Toyama Bay, just after its successful attack on the 5,500 ton freighter, *Konzan Maru.* Working the western side of the Sea off Korea, *Flying Fish, Bowfin,* and *Tinosa* sank eight more freighters.

The eight surviving submarines rendezvoused at the north end of the Sea of Japan on the night of June 24th and raced together on the surface in a dense fog through La Perouse Strait. Altogether the attack cost the Empire 27 merchantmen and one submarine, and seriously disrupted the last major supply line to Japan.

The FM Sonar Mine Detector (right). In April 1943 Admiral Charles Lockwood visited the Naval Research Laboratory at San Diego. Scientists demonstrated a new type of Frequency Modulated (FM) sonar, originally developed to locate mines for surface minesweepers. Because it gave bearing information on underwater objects just as radar did on the surface, the scientists suggested that submerged submarines could use it for mine detection. Lockwood saw its potential, and the first experimental set went to war on *Tinosa* in late 1944. By May 1945, nine submarines were equipped with detectors and ready to invade the Sea of Japan in "Operation Barney."

FM Sonar Mine Detector

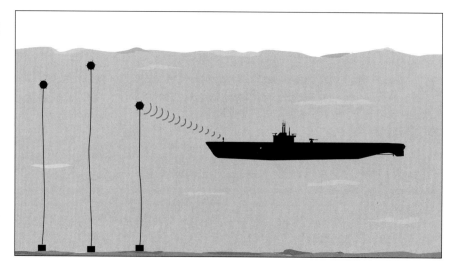

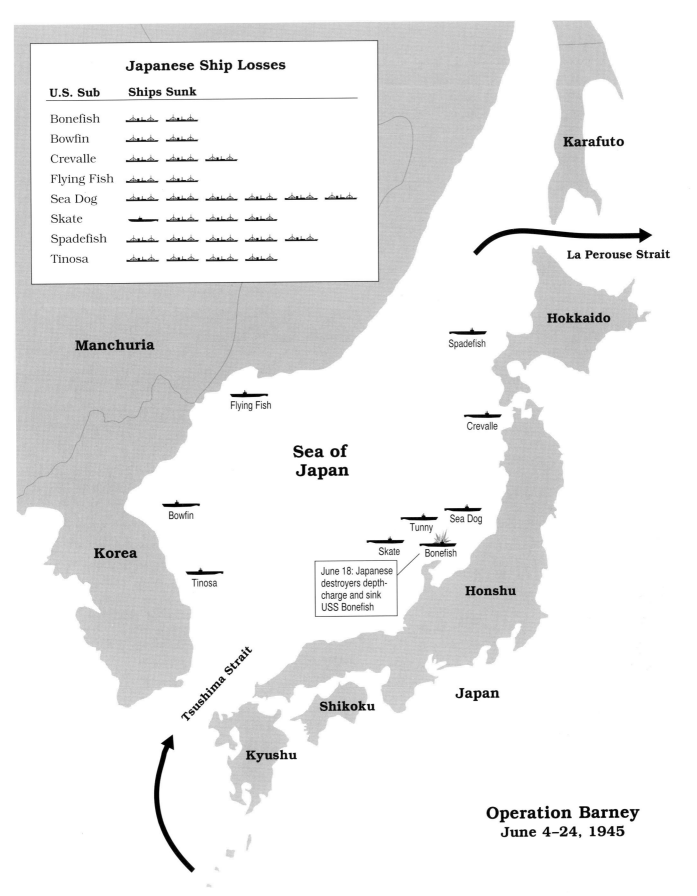

Japanese Ship Losses

U.S. Sub	Ships Sunk
Bonefish	🚢🚢
Bowfin	🚢🚢
Crevalle	🚢🚢🚢
Flying Fish	🚢🚢
Sea Dog	🚢🚢🚢🚢🚢🚢
Skate	🚢🚢🚢🚢
Spadefish	🚢🚢🚢🚢🚢
Tinosa	🚢🚢🚢🚢

Karafuto

La Perouse Strait

Hokkaido

Spadefish

Manchuria

Flying Fish

Crevalle

**Sea of
Japan**

Bowfin

Sea Dog

Tunny

Skate

Bonefish

June 18: Japanese
destroyers depth-
charge and sink
USS Bonefish

Korea

Tinosa

Honshu

Tsushima Strait

Japan

Shikoku

Kyushu

Operation Barney
June 4–24, 1945

Silent Hunter

Three years to the month after American submarines evacuated U.S. military personnel from besieged Corregidor in the Philippines, Japanese submarines attempted the same mission from the port of Aparri in northern Luzon. In February 1945, General MacArthur's forces dislodged the Imperial Army north of Manila and important Japanese officials wanted to escape. The Imperial Navy ordered four submarines—*RO-45*, *RO-55*, *RO-112* and *RO-113*—to ferry ammunition from Formosa to Luzon and then evacuate key people.

American codebreakers at Pearl Harbor eavesdropped on the plan and Admiral Lockwood directed six U.S. submarines in the South China Sea to intercept the rescue. One of these subs was USS *Batfish* on its sixth war patrol. *Batfish*, commanded by Captain John K. Fyfe, had spent the previous two weeks fighting a typhoon, avoiding fishing junks, and looking for targets in an empty sea.

At 10:10 p.m. on the night of February 9th, while patrolling the Babuyan Channel just north of Luzon, *Batfish* detected an enemy radar signal. Captain Fyfe ordered the submarine to battle stations

to conduct a night surface radar attack. At 11:30 *Batfish* fired four torpedoes, but all missed. Thirty minutes later the boat fired three more torpedoes and sank the Japanese submarine *RO-55*, making its escape from Aparri with a crew of 45 and 42 passengers.

The next night at 7:15 p.m. in the same area, *Batfish* picked up a similar radar signal. Once again Captain Fyfe started his attack, but the Japanese submarine dived before torpedoes could be fired. *Batfish* swung away and a half hour later its sound system detected the blowing ballast tanks of a surfacing submarine. *Batfish* approached at radar depth and at 10:02 p.m. torpedoed and sank *RO-112* with all hands.

Two days later at 2 a.m. on February 13th, the incredulous Americans picked up yet another radar signal. *Batfish* closed on the contact at radar depth, but the Japanese submarine chose this moment to dive. The U.S. sub waited in the area and an hour later the enemy submarine surfaced and continued on its previous course. Captain Fyfe closed

in at radar depth and at 4:49 a.m. fired three torpedoes at *RO-113*. The first torpedo blew up the Japanese submarine so completely that the next two passed through the wreckage without exploding. The next morning *Batfish* recovered a small wooden box containing navigational equipment and a book of tables in the oil slick that marked *RO-113*'s grave.

Batfish (bottom), commissioned on August 21, 1943, made its first two patrols under Lt. Comdr. Wayne Merrill and sank one cargo ship. John Fyfe took command for *Batfish*'s next four patrols. The sub sank another freighter and four warships, and rescued three Allied airmen. *Batfish* completed seven patrols during the war and received official credit for six ships, including three RO class submarines.

North of the Philippines February 1945

Babuyan Islands

Babuyan Island

Calayan

Feb. 13, 4:49 a.m.: Batfish sinks submarine, RO-113

Dalupiri

Feb. 11, 10:02 p.m.: Batfish sinks submarine, RO-112

Feb. 10, 12:00 a.m.: Batfish sinks submarine, RO-55

Camiguin

Fuga

Aparri

N

Luzon

Lt. Comdr. Koichiro Suwa commanded submarine *RO-55* on its last mission—to deliver ammunition and rescue important civilians from Luzon. Lt. Comdr. Jun Yuji in *RO-112* attempted to bring ammunition into Aparri and to evacuate stranded airmen. *RO-113*, under command of Kiyoshi Harada, was also trying to deliver ammunition when it was sunk by USS *Batfish.* U.S. submarines sank 23 of the 134 submarines the Japanese lost during the war.

Quartermaster John Glace (below) in *Batfish's* forward torpedo room sews victory flags to commemorate the sinking of three Japanese submarines. A flag with a rising sun signified a sunken warship and a flag with a red sun on a white field indicated a merchant ship sunk.

Batfish's Battle Flags

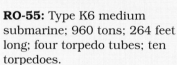

RO-55: Type K6 medium submarine; 960 tons; 264 feet long; four torpedo tubes; ten torpedoes.

RO-112: Type KS medium submarine; 525 tons; 200 feet long; four torpedo tubes, eight torpedoes.

RO-113: Type KS medium submarine; 525 tons; speed: 14 knots on surface, eight knots submerged.

The Final Attack

The war was almost over—almost. At the beginning of August 1945 USS *Torsk* sailed from Guam on its second war patrol. Using FM sonar to detect mines, *Torsk* safely passed through Tsushima Strait and entered the Sea of Japan. On its first day in the Sea, August 11th, the submarine picked up seven Japanese merchant seamen clinging to a life raft. They told the Americans that their small cargo ship, the *Koue Maru*, had been sunk by U.S. fighter planes four days earlier.

The *Torsk's* captain, Bafford E. Lewellen, who had commanded the *Pollack* in 1943 and sunk eight ships, continued the patrol and at 8:30 a.m. on August 12th sank a small freighter—*Torsk's* first victory. The sub duplicated the performance the next day, August 13th, by sinking another freighter, *Kaiho Maru.* However, a larger cargo ship managed to escape into a nearby harbor.

A few miles up the coast on August 14th, *Torsk* sighted this cargo ship underway with an escort. Commander Lewellen decided to tackle the escort first. He fired a small acoustic homing torpedo, nicknamed by the sailors "cutie," and sank *Kaikoban No. 13.* In the confusion the cargo ship slipped into a local harbor and another escort vessel came out looking for the *Torsk.* Lewellen missed with his first "cutie" torpedo, but the second one ran true and down went *Kaikoban No. 47.* Unknown to *Torsk's* captain or crew, they had sunk the last Japanese ship of the war.

A sand bar prevented an attack on the freighter in the harbor and *Torsk* retired from the area.That night the submarine received the fleet-wide message from Admiral Chester Nimitz: "Cease offensive operations against Japanese forces." World War II was over.

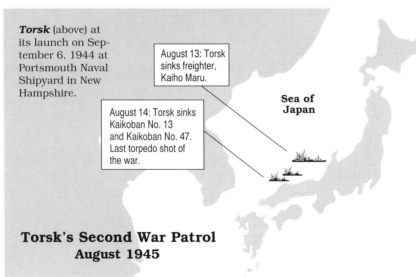

Torsk (above) at its launch on September 6, 1944 at Portsmouth Naval Shipyard in New Hampshire.

August 13: Torsk sinks freighter, Kaiho Maru.

August 14: Torsk sinks Kaikoban No. 13 and Kaikoban No. 47. Last torpedo shot of the war.

Sea of Japan

**Torsk's Second War Patrol
August 1945**

Ye Olde Torske
Torche (left) was the submarine *Torsk's* weekly newspaper. Radiomen Charles "Wahoo" Waugh and Ervin Schmidt published it on the ship's typewriter, using six sheets of onion-skin paper interlaced with carbon sheets. Seven copies were thus produced and posted into each major compartment. The newsletter recounted recent events aboard the submarine, news from Pearl Harbor, gossip, and humor. On September 4, 1945 the *Torche* reported: "The censorship of personal mail has been discontinued effective immediately, so you all can again carry on your love life in private.... [This] does not mean that the lid is off and you are now free to write about anything you may desire. It is merely a recognition of the fact that you would like a little more privacy and the censors would like a little more drinking time."

T·H·E * I·M·P·A·R·T·I·A·L * U·N·C·E·N·S·O·R·E·D * T·R·U·T·H!

"YE OLDE TORSKE TORCHE"

* * * * * * *

AUGUST 14,1945 - Torske County USA (JAPANESE SEA)

FLASH!!!!! FLASH!!!!! U.S.S. TORSK SINKS TWO ENEMY MEN-OF-WAR..

Immediately following receipt of the foregoing dispatch, an official communique from B.E. Lewellen, Skipper of the rampaging submarine Torsk disclosed that his vessel had encountered, and sunk, two enemy warships during an exciting engagement in the Sea of Japan. Details of the sinkings, as glowingly described by the victor of the soul-stirring sea-duel, follow.

The first attack was made on a frigate which was escorting a freighter along the coast. We were inshore of the frigate and between him and the freighter. One torpedo lifted his stern about thirty degrees in the air and stopped him cold.

We then turned our attention to the freighter.... While we were working around to get him lined up with the harbor entrance, our first target rolled over and sank. Very shortly thereafter, however, more echo ranging was heard, and another one of the same type came into view over the horizon. He was headed our way; and when he kept on coming, there was nothing left for us to do but let him have one down the throat. This we did, and quickly retired to the depths. After the designated length of time, and there was no explosion, we let go with the other barrel. No sooner had we fired than there was a very satisfactory Bang! and all screw noises and echo ranging ceased. A second explosion, shortly after the first, indicated that both our torpedoes may have hit. Anyhow, everyone, including myself, breathed a big sigh of relief.... * * * * * * *

EXTRA--EXTRA--EXTRA--EXTRA--EXTRA--EXTRA--EXTRA--EXTRA--EXTRA

!!!!!FLASH!!FLASH!!!!!

JAPAN ACCEPTS SURRENDER TERMS, (WEDNESDAY, AUGUST 15, 1945).

President Truman announced at seven o'clock, tonight, Japanese acceptance of surrender terms proclaimed at the Potsdam conference. The terms will be accepted by General MacArthur "Dug-out-Dug" when arrangements can be completed.

Mr. Truman read the formal message, relayed from Emperor Hirohito through the Swiss Government, in which the Japanese ruler pledged the surrender on the terms laid down by the Big Three at Potsdam. President Truman read this statement; "I have received, this afternoon, a message from the Japanese government in reply to a message forwarded to that government by the secretary of state on August eleven. I deem this reply a full acceptance of the Potsdam declaration, which specifies the unconditional surrender of Japan. In this reply there is no

Homeward bound (right) at the end of the war, the crew of the *Torsk* enjoys the warm Pacific sun. After the Japanese surrender on September 2, 1945 a U.S. destroyer escorted *Torsk* out of the mined Sea of Japan. The submarine dropped its seven Japanese POWs at Guam and returned to Pearl Harbor. There, the crew received three days at the Royal Hawaiian Hotel and then sailed to Panama. *Torsk* transited the canal and returned to New London and a great celebration.

Deck of the Missouri

The greatest war in history was over. The Japanese capitulated on August 14th, and the Allies set the formal surrender ceremonies for September 2, 1945 aboard the U.S. battleship *Missouri*, anchored in Tokyo Bay. Hundreds of warships gathered around the *Missouri* that morning, including a representative dozen U.S. submarines.

The Allies made this fitting gesture because a large share of the victory in the Pacific belonged to the U.S. submarine service. Although they represented only two percent of the U.S. Navy, American submarines destroyed 55 percent of all Japanese ships. They sank 1,200 merchantmen and 200 warships. The warships lost to U.S. submarines comprised nearly one-third of the Imperial Navy. This remarkable success came at a high price. Fifty-two of 288 commissioned U.S. submarines were sunk. Thirty-five hundred and five of the 16,000 American submariners who made war patrols never returned—a casualty rate of 22 percent.

Ironically, the secrecy protecting submarine operations during World War II prevented a wide public awareness of their importance, and the U.S. submarine campaign is one of the least known stories of the war. Nevertheless, for the submariners, the love of their ships mixed with the knowledge of their accomplishment created a special pride sustained all their lives. For the record, their victory remains one of the great feats of arms in naval history.

Admiral Chester Nimitz (above) signs the Japanese surrender for the Allies on September 2, 1945. General Douglas MacArthur, Admiral William Halsey, and Rear Admiral Forrest Sherman (left to right) look on from behind.

Sailfish (right) at New London, Connecticut after the war. *Sailfish* sank two Japanese warships and five merchantment during World War II. Happy crew members pose for a photograph, grateful to be home.

The Enlisted Men

The captains gave orders, made the decisions during battle, wrote the reports, and received most of the medals, but the enlisted men ran the ship. They were specialists who submerged and surfaced the submarine in less than a minute, torpedomen who spent hours carefully checking the 24 deadly Mark 14 and Mark 18 torpedoes, machinist's mates who cared for the big Winton diesel engines, electricians who maintained the submarine's electric motors and 252 storage battery cells. Enlisted men manned the radios, sonar, and all-important radar. The cooks prepared three meals a day for 75 men and, in their spare time, provided baked goods to the ever-hungry submariners. A pharmacist's mate repaired the sprains, treated minor wounds, and occasionally faced major injuries caused by the enemy or accidents. Except for lookouts, many of the men never saw the sun from the time the submarine left port until it returned. Conversations, endless games of acey-deucey, reading, and sleeping reduced the boredom and allowed them to get along. It was crowded but they made do. They endured the fear caused by Japanese bombs and depth charges and did their duty.

An enlisted man (above) holds a prize of war—the captured life preserver from the freighter, *Oyama Maru.* The submarine, *Drum,* sank the 3,800 ton cargo ship on April 9, 1943, north of the Bismarck Islands.

William Soczek
Fire Controlman/TDC Operator
USS *Growler*

We heard the destroyer coming. I was alone in the after torpedo room in that single hull because I had a flooded firing circuit. I was sitting on top of the torpedo when he dropped three depth charges. And I'll swear that the bulkhead pushed inward! I looked around. All I could see was that the hatch was shut. The phones were dangling. Everyone had gotten out of there and I was alone. It was a hell of a feeling.

Bill Soczek was born in Pennsylvania and raised in Detroit, Michigan. After high school, in 1938, he enlisted in the Navy and underwent training in surface fire control systems. Following the Pearl Harbor attack, the Navy transferred Soczek to the submarine service to operate the new Torpedo Data Computer (TDC). He joined USS *Growler*, commanded by Howard Gilmore, and headed for the Pacific.

When the Japanese occupied Kiska and Attu in the Aleutian Islands, Admiral Nimitz ordered eight fleet boats, including *Growler*, north to reinforce U.S. positions. Early on the morning of July 5, 1942, a few miles off Kiska, Lt. Comdr. Gilmore sighted three Japanese destroyers at anchor. While Bill Soczek operated the TDC, *Growler* torpedoed all three ships, sinking the *Arare* and damaging *Kasumi* and *Shiranuhi*. Gilmore turned from his periscope after the torpedo hits and ordered Bill Soczek promoted a rank.

On the night of February 7, 1943, while on its fourth war patrol, *Growler* detected a small ship five miles away and maneuvered at 17 knots to attack. Rain squalls confused the radar picture and poor visibility hid the enemy vessel until it loomed up a few hundred yards away on a collision course. Gilmore ordered hard left rudder but *Growler* struck the supply vessel, *Hayasaki*, amidships. *Growler's* bow crumpled and the submarine heeled over and threw everyone off their feet. The Japanese sprayed machine gun fire over the ship which sounded like a "swarm of angry bees" to Soczek in the conning tower. The wounded Captain Gilmore, still on the bridge, ordered "Take her down!" *Growler* submerged and crept away to make repairs.

Bill Soczek went on to become chief of the boat and served aboard *Growler* for its first nine patrols. *Growler* was lost with all hands on its 11th war patrol.

Early in 1944 Bill Soczek was scheduled to replace a sailor on USS *Trout* who was going on leave to see his wife in the States. The day before *Trout* left Midway the sailor received a divorce letter and decided to stay aboard. *Trout* was lost with all hands two weeks later while attacking a troop convoy.

The Enlisted Men

**Charles E. Stewart
Signalman
USS _R-6_, USS _Cutlass_**

_R-6_ at sea
(above). The R-class submarine, launched just after World War I, was 186 feet long and displaced 570 tons. The sub mounted four 18-inch torpedo tubes and carried eight torpedoes. Two officers and 27 enlisted men manned the boat. It could sail 13 knots on the surface and 10 knots underwater. _R-6_ served as a training boat in World War II.

The last words my mother said to me when I left for the Navy were, "Don't go near an airplane or a submarine."

Chuck Stewart was born and raised in Washington state's Puget Sound region. He joined the Navy in April 1942 and went to boot camp in Idaho. At an instructor's suggestion, he took a 16-week signal course at the University of Chicago. Unknown to Stewart and his fellow sailors as they practiced Morse code in the stands at the University's Stagg Field, a few hundred yards away Enrico Fermi and other Manhattan Project scientists were constructing the world's first atomic reactor.

Stewart graduated as a signalman third class and faced assignment to a gun crew on a tanker headed for Murmansk. He saw a notice asking for volunteers for the submarine service and decided this was a better way to get to the war. In New London, Connecticut he took the 12-week training course in submarines.

On his first day at sub school he went aboard an old 1917–18 O-class boat for a test dive. When the boat quietly slipped beneath the waves Stewart thought to himself, "This is the greatest thing since the wheel." Upon graduation he requested a fleet boat but the Navy ordered him to the old _R-6_, based on the Atlantic coast. Stewart spent the next 15 months aboard _R-6_, training anti-submarine forces in sub detection.

Desperate to get a fleet boat before the war ended, he convinced his captain to give him a transfer. The Navy assigned him to the _Cutlass_, which sailed to the Pacific in mid-1945 and made one patrol off the coast of Japan. By this time enemy shipping had largely disappeared and _Cutlass_ spent its time dodging the abundant Japanese mines and radar-equipped patrol planes.

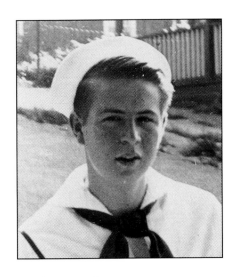

**Tudor Davis
Torpedoman
USS *Halibut***

Tudor Davis grew up in Pottsville, Pennsylvania, a coal mining town 90 miles north of Philadelphia. After a six-month stint in the Civilian Conservation Corps, he joined the Navy in October 1941 at the age of 17. Davis spent the next year aboard the heavy cruiser, *Tuscaloosa*, making three North Atlantic convoy runs to Murmansk. In July 1942 his convoy, PQ-17, lost 22 out of 33 ships to combined German U-boat and *Luftwaffe* attacks.

Davis transferred to submarine school in December 1942 and after completing the course, joined USS *Halibut* in Pearl Harbor as a torpedoman. He served aboard *Halibut* for six war patrols, until the sub was heavily damaged on November 14, 1944 in Luzon Strait. On that day Captain Pete Galantin attacked a heavily escorted convoy. Using an airborne magnetic detector, Japanese planes located the submerged *Halibut* and dropped bombs and dye markers to mark the ship's location. Surface vessels then delivered a tremendous depth charge barrage that almost sank the submarine. One string of charges exploded just above the four-inch

I spent my first year in the Navy aboard the heavy cruiser, USS Tuscaloosa. We made three runs to Murmansk, escorting convoys, and then took part in the invasion of North Africa. I wanted to leave the Tuscaloosa because I didn't like bosun's mates and their whistles telling me what to do from 5:30 a.m. to midnight. Also, my cousin, who joined the Navy at the same time, went directly into submarines. He wrote me in October 1942 as a machinist's mate, while I was still a seaman 2nd class. So I decided instead of watching these torpedoes go by, I was going to shoot them.

deck gun. The blast forced the submarine down several hundred feet even as it rippled the steel hull like a washboard. In the forward torpedo room, torpedo skids ripped away from the bulkhead when a dozen one-inch bolts shattered. Only a miracle kept the torpedoes from crushing the crew.

Captain Galantin brought *Halibut* and a grateful Tudor Davis to the surface four hours later to find the Japanese gone. Escorted by USS *Pintado*, the *Halibut* limped back to Pearl Harbor and then to the Portsmouth Navy Yard

where it was determined the submarine could not be repaired. Admiral Lockwood wrote, "The stellar performance by the men of the *Halibut* saved this ship from destruction." Tudor Davis ended the war in New London, awaiting assignment to another sub.

The forward torpedo room (below). Loading torpedoes before a war patrol required a full day's work from the torpedomen. Sixteen "fish" were brought through the forward torpedo loading hatch at a 45° angle, one at a time. Six went into the tubes and ten more were placed on skids.

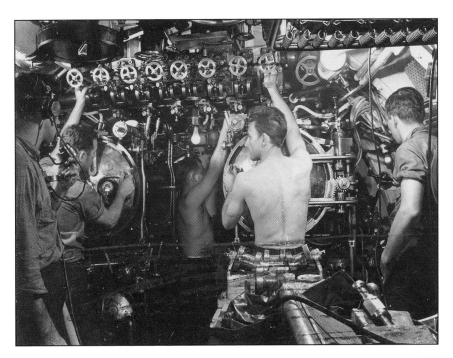

The Enlisted Men

**John Fankhauser
Torpedoman
USS *Porpoise***

I was on lookout. It was a dark night. Complete overcast. No stars, nothing. I saw something that looked dark on the horizon and then it turned light. And I reported it to the officer on deck. . . . It turned out to be a target—an enemy submarine. When I came off watch, the captain called me into the wardroom. He said, "I was unhappy with you a while ago. I changed my mind. As of now, you're one rank higher."

John Fankhauser was raised in northern Washington state. He graduated from high school in 1929 and spent most of the Great Depression working as a lumberman. On the weekend of December 7, 1941, he went home to go duck hunting. When he returned from the shoot his father told him the Japanese had attacked the U.S. Fleet at Pearl Harbor.

Fankhauser joined the Navy and was sent to boot camp and then torpedo school in San Diego. After graduation he volunteered for submarines and the Navy ordered him to the USS *Porpoise*, which had just finished an overhaul at Mare Island Naval Ship Yard.

Fankhauser soon found himself at sea on his first war patrol. Standing lookout one night, he spotted an enemy submarine and although *Porpoise* was unable to develop an attack, the commander promoted him one rank. *Porpoise* continued on to Japan, and on New Year's Day torpedoed two freighters, sinking one and running the other ship aground. The destroyer escort dropped a dozen depth charges which loosened *Porpoise's* rivets and started an oil leak. The damage forced the submarine back to Pearl Harbor for repairs before continuing its patrol to Truk. Upon returning, a new skipper, Carter Bennett, assumed command and once again *Porpoise* turned its bow toward the south Pacific.

The new captain made three attacks, sinking a transport and damaging two freighters. A subsequent depth-charging caused the old oil leak to return and Bennett took the sub back to Pearl Harbor. The Navy decided *Porpoise* should be taken out of combat and sent to New London to serve as a training boat. John Fankhauser went with the *Porpoise* and served aboard it until the end of the war.

Porpoise (right) at sea. The Navy commissioned *Porpoise* in August 1935. The sub began the war as part of the U.S. Asiatic Fleet and received official credit for sinking three cargo ships.

Donald Naze
Chief Torpedoman
USS _Seawolf_

Donald Naze grew up in Jamestown, North Dakota. He enlisted in the Navy in April 1940 at the age of 21 and after boot camp served on the submarine tender USS _Beaver_. Not long afterward he volunteered for submarine duty and was sent first to submarine school in New London, Connecticut and then to torpedo training in Rhode Island.

Upon completion of the course, the Navy sent him to the submarine shipyard at Manitowoc, Wisconsin to join a new boat, the USS _Pogy_. The submarine set out from Pearl Harbor on its first war patrol off the northeastern coast of Honshu, Japan in April 1943. _Pogy_ sank a gunboat and a merchant ship in these heavily mined waters and returned safely. Two other U.S. submarines, however, _Pickerel_ and _Runner_, were lost in the same area, probably due to mines.

Using Ultra code information on its second war patrol in August, _Pogy_ intercepted and

I am now a chief torpedoman, as of June 15th, so you all have a treat on me and send me the bill. Ha! Ha!
— *letter home, July 10, 1944*

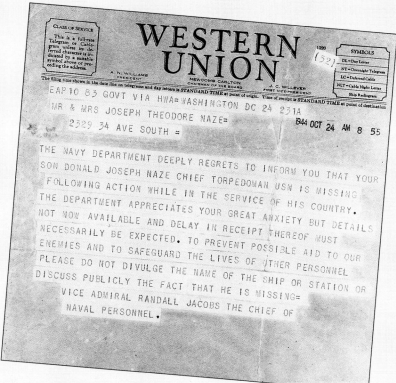

sank the 7,400 ton aircraft ferry, _Mogamigawa Maru_, near Truk. _Pogy_ went on to sink a total of 16 ships by the end of the war.

After this patrol, Donald Naze transferred to the famous submarine, USS _Seawolf_. The sub left on its 11th war patrol in October 1943 and sank two merchantmen, _Fusei Maru_ and _Wuhu Maru_, off Hong Kong. The submarine returned to this area on its 12th patrol and attacked a seven-ship convoy. In a grueling daylong battle on January 16th, Capt. Royce L. Gross and torpedoman Donald Naze sank four large Japanese freighters.

After this outstanding patrol _Seawolf_ returned to Mare Island, California for refit and Naze went on leave. He spent three weeks with his wife Etta in Providence, Rhode Island and then visited his parents for the first time in four years.

Seawolf returned to the Pacific and began to ferry guerrillas to the Philippines in preparation for the U.S. invasion. On October 3, 1944 the American destroyer, _Richard M. Rowell_ mistook the submerged _Seawolf_ for a Japanese submarine and sank the ship with all hands.

The Enlisted Men

**Ralph Van Horn
Motor Machinist's Mate
USS *Flasher***

My main duties on Flasher *were as a throttle-man, operating and maintaining two Winton V-16 main engines and two Kleinschmidt electric water distillers—making drinking and battery waters.*

Ralph Van Horn was born and raised in Suffern, New York. Upon graduation from high school in 1940 he enlisted in the Navy and volunteered for the submarine service. The Navy assigned him to an S-boat, the *S-12*, based at the Panama Canal zone. He earned his dolphins on the old submarine.

In June 1943 Van Horn transferred to USS *Flasher,* then under construction. The Navy commissioned *Flasher* on September 25th of that year and Ralph Van Horn reported aboard. As a motor machinist's mate, he maintained two of *Flasher's* 1,600 horsepower diesel engines. During battle surface attacks he ran to the bridge and passed ammunition canisters up through the hatch and down to the waiting gun crew.

Flasher sailed on its first war patrol at the beginning of 1944 under veteran Captain Reuben Whitaker. The submarine sank its second ship, a freighter, on February 5th and then surfaced to attack three accompanying motor sampans. Ralph Van Horn celebrated his 22nd birthday that night, passing ammunition up the hatch to sink one sampan and damage two others.

He stayed aboard *Flasher* for its first four war patrols in which the submarine sank 18 ships (14

officially). On his third patrol he was upgraded to motor machinist's mate first class.

Ralph Van Horn transferred to New London, Connecticut in February 1945 for assignment to the *Cubera,* a new submarine under construction. The war ended before the ship could be commissioned and he received an honorable discharge in October 1945.

***Flasher* at its** launching (below) on June 20, 1943 at the Electric Boat Company in Groton, Connecticut. Lt Comdr. Reuben Whitaker took command three months later. Whitaker began the war in Manila as executive officer of *Sturgeon*. He served as captain of *S-44* for one patrol, and then transferred to the *Flying Fish* as executive officer for another patrol. Whitaker, an outstanding officer, sank 14 enemy ships while commanding *Flasher*.

I got off watch after midnight and then up at 7:30 in time to get breakfast before the eight-to-noon watch, which was followed by the eight-to-midnight watch. It kept me up about 18 hours a day. Occasionally, I got a short nap in the afternoon. That didn't happen too frequently because there were many electrical repairs that needed my attention.

**Pete Mitchell
Electrician's Mate
USS *Flying Fish*, USS *Tinosa***

Pete Mitchell grew up in the beautiful hills of eastern Washington. The eldest son, he helped his father raise his two sisters and brother after his mother passed away. Upon leaving high school, he worked for several months in a lumber mill before enlisting in the Navy in 1929 at the age of 17. Mitchell went to boot camp in San Diego and then was assigned to the aircraft carrier, USS *Lexington*. Almost immediately, the Navy reassigned the young sailor to duty with the voters' commission in Nicaragua where U.S. Marines were organizing elections while battling guerrillas led by Cesar Augusto Sandino.

When he returned home in 1932 he requested sub duty. The Navy transferred him to the submarine school at New London, Connecticut. After graduation he joined the submarine, *Argonaut*, based at Pearl Harbor, where he completed electrical training and became an electrician's mate third class. Pete Mitchell loved the casual prewar duty in Hawaii, but in 1937 the Navy transferred him to a new boat, the *Pompano*, under construction at Mare Island, California. He spent four years on *Pompano* before moving to another new submarine, the *Flying Fish*.

After the Pearl Harbor attack, the Navy accelerated submarine training and *Flying Fish* put to sea on April 6, 1942. The boat arrived at Midway Island on May 21st, in time to join the submarine screen that protected the outpost during the carrier air battle (June 3–4, 1942). When the Japanese retreated, *Flying Fish* conducted its first patrol to the East China Sea, but found no targets. In August, ComSubPac sent the submarine to Truk to intercept Japanese reinforcements converging on Guadalcanal. *Flying Fish*, commanded by Donc Donaho, torpedoed and damaged a Kongo-class battleship on August 28th. Six days later, the sub sank a patrol boat. This brought on a depth charge attack that lasted four and a half hours and seriously damaged *Flying Fish*.

Arriving safely back at Pearl Harbor, the Navy transferred Pete Mitchell to the USS *Tinosa*. He made two runs on the *Tinosa* before going to a new boat, the USS *Ronquil*, in Portsmouth, New Hampshire. *Ronquil* arrived in the Pacific in July 1944 with Warrant Officer Mitchell aboard, and left on the last day of the month for its first war patrol. The *Ronquil* sank two large cargo ships off Formosa and then put into Majuro Atoll in the Marshall Islands for refit.

The Navy promoted Pete Mitchell to lieutenant (j.g.) and sent him to the USS *Sawfish* for its ninth patrol. He finished the war in San Diego, serving on the training boat, *S-33*.

USS *Tinosa* (left) steams into its berth at Pearl Harbor after a 1945 war patrol to the Sea of Japan. The small Japanese flags displayed on the submarine represent the number of ships sunk on the patrol.

The Enlisted Men

Joe Phenneger
Motor Machinist's Mate
USS Kingfish

On the Marshall Islands, the U.S. sub tender, Fulton, thought the sub tender, Sperry, was feeding us, and the Sperry thought the Fulton was feeding us. It ended up the only things we ate for nearly a week were the fish we caught and the coconuts we picked in the jungle. To this day, I still don't like the sound of the milk shaking around in the coconuts.

Joe Phenneger was born into a farming family in Bentley, Kansas in 1921. After graduation from high school, he joined the Navy and went to Great Lakes Boot Camp and then to diesel school at the Navy Pier in Chicago. A landing ship tank vessel took him from Mare Island to Pearl Harbor and there he transferred to the submarine tender, USS *Sperry.*

The *Sperry* set up support operations at Majuro in the Marshall Islands and Phenneger began serving in submarine relief crews. When a call came for new men to volunteer for sub duty he joined the veteran boat, USS *Kingfish.*

On May 1, 1944 Motor Machinist's Mate Joe Phenneger and the submarine left on its eighth war patrol. The ship made a uneventful voyage to the Bonin Islands before going back to Mare Island for a complete overhaul.

Four months later, *Kingfish* set off for the east coast of Japan where it sank three cargo ships. The submarine went to Guam for supplies, and just before Christmas 1944 headed once again for the Japanese coast. *Kingfish* sank two more freighters on this patrol, and on the next one rescued four Royal Navy pilots who had been shot down.

Joe Phenneger and *Kingfish* arrived at Midway on August 14, 1945 two hours before the war ended, in time to take part in the considerable celebration.

***Kingfish's* crew** (right) next to a captured Japanese midget submarine at Camp Sam Dealey on Guam. The U.S. Navy set up a submarine rest camp on Guam in October 1944 and named it in honor of the lost *Harder's* captain.

Battle flags flying, (right opposite) a U.S. submarine heads home to Hawaii at the end of the war.

After the Pearl Harbor attack, three or four days went by before I got ahold of a postcard to let my parents know I was alive. It took the card two weeks to get to Wisconsin. Meanwhile, I had been reported missing. Our church in Marshfield gave me a beautiful funeral. As far as my folks knew, I was dead. Then one night a few days later, my mother was in the barn, milking, and she was leaning against the cow, crying, when she suddenly became aware of a horn blowing way off in the distance. It kept getting closer. Finally, the mailman came down the road, blowing his horn all the way. He drove up the driveway, right into the barn. While sorting the mail, he'd run across my card and discovered I was alive.

**Ervin Schmidt
Radioman
USS *Saury*, USS *Torsk***

Ervin Schmidt's family immigrated to the United States from Germany in 1923 when he was seven years old. They settled in Marshfield, Wisconsin and started a dairy farm. After high school Ervin worked on the farm, did two stints in the Civilian Conservation Corps, and studied to be a barber. In the summer of 1940 he joined the Navy and trained as a radioman. The service assigned him to the battleship, USS *California*, which moved to Pearl Harbor, Hawaii in late 1940.

On the morning of December 7, 1941 Ervin was preparing to go to church when the General Quarters alarm announced the beginning of the Japanese attack. Two torpedoes slammed into *California* and the battleship gradually sank. Overcome by fumes, Ervin survived only because other crewmen carried him to up the deck.

Ervin Schmidt and 150 other *California* sailors joined the heavy cruiser, *Chicago*, several days later and sailed for the South Pacific. *Chicago* took part in the invasion of Guadalcanal and had its bow blown off on the night of August 9, 1942, during the Battle of Savo Island. After repairs, *Chicago* returned to the Solomons campaign in January 1943 and was sunk by Japanese torpedo planes.

Tired of having ships sunk from beneath him, Ervin volunteered for submarine duty and joined the crew of the *Saury*. He made four patrols before transferring to a new boat, USS *Torsk*. The *Torsk* made its first patrol in the Sea of Japan. On August 14, 1945, it sank two attacking frigates and fired the last torpedoes of the war. Ervin Schmidt had the distinction of being at Pearl Harbor and aboard the ship which fired the last shots of World War II.

U.S. Submarine Losses

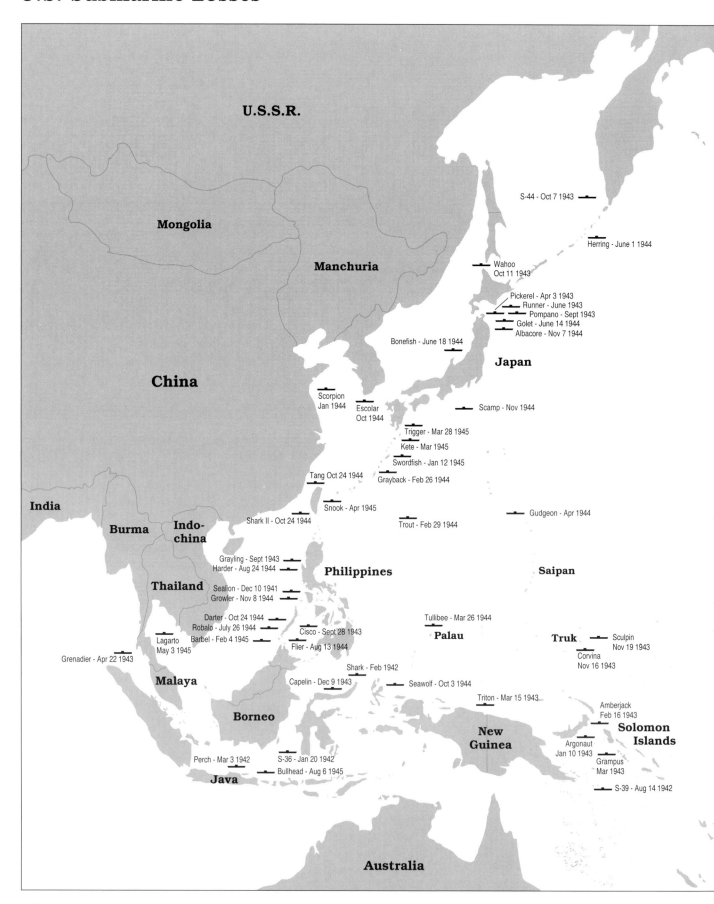

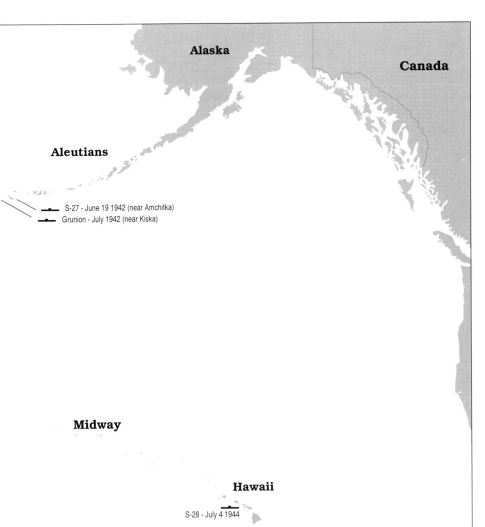

S-27 - June 19 1942 (near Amchitka)
Grunion - July 1942 (near Kiska)

S-28 - July 4 1944

R-12 - June 12 1943

Dorado - Oct 12 1943

S-26 - Jan 24 1942

The United States Navy lost 52 submarines and 3,505 submariners in World War II. This casualty rate of approximately 22 percent was the highest of all the services, and was six times greater than in the surface navy.

Sealion was the first U.S. submarine lost in the war, a victim of Japanese bombs at Cavite Navy Yard on December 10, 1941. The new year, 1942, found American submarines in action throughout the Pacific, but casualties remained low. Two S-boats sank in January. The Navy lost two fleet submarines in the hard fighting around the Dutch East Indies in February and March, and a fleet boat and two S-boats in the summer. A total of seven submarines went down in 1942.

The pace of the war quickened in 1943 and U.S. submarine losses increased. The Japanese destroyed *Argonaut* on January 10, 1943, and thereafter one or two U.S. submarines were sunk each month. The year 1943 ended with the loss of 17 U.S. submarines. All but four went down with their entire crews.

Japanese ship casualties soared and the heavy fighting claimed new American victims. The submarine *Scorpion* vanished in the Yellow Sea—probably due to a mine—in January 1944. Famous boats such as *Trout*, *Harder*, *Seawolf*, *Albacore*, and *Scamp* failed to return from patrols. *Growler* disappeared in November 1944 and brought the number of U.S. submarines destroyed that year to 19.

In January 1945 *Swordfish*, which had sunk the first confirmed Japanese ship a week after Pearl Harbor, perished off Okinawa. Seven more U.S. submarines went down in the final months of the war, bringing 1945 sinkings to eight boats and total losses for the war to 52.

U.S. Submarines in World War II

Submarine Name & Number		Date Commissioned	Submarine Name & Number		Date Commissioned
Albacore*	SS 218	June 1, 1942	Drum	SS 228	November 1, 1941
Amberjack*	SS 219	June 19, 1942	Entemedor	SS 340	April 6, 1945
Angler	SS 240	October 1, 1943	Escolar*	SS 294	June 2, 1944
Apogon	SS 308	July 16, 1943	Finback	SS 230	January 31, 1942
Archerfish	SS 311	September 4, 1943	Flasher	SS 249	September 25, 1943
Argonaut*	SS 166	April 2, 1928	Flier*	SS 250	October 18, 1943
Argonaut II	SS 475	January 15, 1945	Flounder	SS 251	November 29, 1943
Aspro	SS 309	July 31, 1943	Flying Fish	SS 229	December 10, 1941
Atule	SS 403	June 21, 1944	Gabilan	SS 252	December 28, 1943
Balao	SS 285	February 4, 1943	Gar	SS 206	April 14, 1941
Bang	SS 385	December 4, 1943	Gato	SS 212	December 31, 1941
Barb	SS 220	July 8, 1942	Golet*	SS 361	November 30, 1943
Barbel*	SS 316	April 3, 1944	Grampus*	SS 207	May 23, 1941
Barbero	SS 317	April 29, 1944	Grayback*	SS 208	June 30, 1941
Bashaw	SS 241	October 25, 1943	Grayling*	SS 209	March 1, 1941
Batfish	SS 310	August 21, 1943	Greenling	SS 213	January 21, 1942
Baya	SS 318	May 20, 1944	Grenadier*	SS 210	May 1, 1941
Becuna	SS 319	May 27, 1944	Grouper	SS 214	February 12, 1942
Bergall	SS 320	June 12, 1944	Growler*	SS 215	March 20, 1942
Besugo	SS 321	June 19, 1944	Grunion*	SS 216	April 11, 1942
Billfish	SS 286	April 20, 1943	Guardfish	SS 217	May 8, 1942
Blackfin	SS 322	July 4, 1944	Guavina	SS 362	December 23, 1943
Blackfish	SS 221	July 22, 1942	Gudgeon*	SS 211	April 21, 1941
Blenny	SS 324	July 27, 1944	Guitarro	SS 363	January 26, 1944
Blower	SS 325	August 10, 1944	Gunnel	SS 253	August 20, 1942
Blueback	SS 326	August 28, 1944	Gurnard	SS 254	September 18, 1942
Bluefish	SS 222	May 24, 1943	Hackleback	SS 295	November 7, 1944
Bluegill	SS 242	November 11, 1943	Haddo	SS 255	October 9, 1942
Boarfish	SS 327	September 23, 1944	Haddock	SS 231	March 14, 1942
Bonefish*	SS 223	May 31, 1943	Hake	SS 256	October 30, 1942
Bowfin	SS 287	May 1, 1943	Halibut	SS 232	April 10, 1942
Bream	SS 243	January 24, 1944	Hammerhead	SS 364	March 1, 1944
Brill	SS 330	October 26, 1944	Harder*	SS 257	December 2, 1942
Bugara	SS 331	November 15, 1944	Hardhead	SS 365	April 18, 1944
Bullhead*	SS 332	December 4, 1944	Hawkbill	SS 366	May 17, 1944
Bumper	SS 333	December 9, 1944	Herring*	SS 233	May 4, 1942
Burrfish	SS 312	September 13, 1943	Hoe	SS 258	December 16, 1942
Cabezon	SS 334	December 30, 1944	Icefish	SS 367	June 10, 1944
Cabrilla	SS 288	May 24, 1943	Jack	SS 259	January 6, 1943
Cachalot	SS 170	December 1, 1933	Jallao	SS 368	July 8, 1944
Caiman	SS 323	July 17, 1944	Kete*	SS 369	July 31, 1944
Capelin*	SS 289	June 4, 1943	Kingfish	SS 234	May 20, 1942
Capitaine	SS 336	January 26, 1945	Kraken	SS 370	September 8, 1944
Carbonero	SS 337	February 7, 1945	Lagarto*	SS 371	October 14, 1944
Carp	SS 338	February 28, 1945	Lamprey	SS 372	November 17, 1944
Catfish	SS 339	March 19, 1945	Lapon	SS 260	January 23, 1943
Cavalla	SS 244	February 29, 1944	Ling	SS 297	June 8, 1945
Cero	SS 225	July 4, 1943	Lionfish	SS 298	November 1, 1944
Charr	SS 328	September 23, 1944	Lizardfish	SS 373	December 30, 1944
Chub	SS 329	October 21, 1944	Loggerhead	SS 374	February 9, 1945
Cisco*	SS 290	May 10, 1943	Macabi	SS 375	March 29, 1945
Clamagore	SS 343	June 28, 1945	Mackerel	SS 204	March 31, 1941
Cobia	SS 245	March 29, 1944	Marlin	SS 205	August 1, 1941
Cod	SS 224	June 21, 1943	Manta	SS 299	December 18, 1944
Corvina*	SS 226	August 6, 1943	Mingo	SS 261	February 12, 1943
Crevalle	SS 291	June 24, 1943	Moray	SS 300	January 26, 1945
Croaker	SS 246	April 21, 1944	Muskallunge	SS 262	March 15, 1943
Cutlass	SS 478	March 17, 1945	Narwhal	SS 167	May 15, 1930
Cuttlefish	SS 171	June 8, 1934	Nautilus	SS 168	July 1, 1930
Dace	SS 247	July 23, 1943	Paddle	SS 263	March 29, 1943
Darter*	SS 227	September 7, 1943	Pampanito	SS 383	November 6, 1943
Dentuda	SS 335	December 30, 1944	Parche	SS 384	November 20, 1943
Devilfish	SS 292	September 1, 1944	Pargo	SS 264	April 26, 1943
Dolphin	SS 169	June 1, 1932	Perch*	SS176	November 19, 1936
Dorado*	SS 248	August 28, 1943	Perch II	SS 313	January 7, 1944
Dragonet	SS 293	March 6, 1944	Permit	SS 178	March 17, 1937

Submarine Name & Number		Date Commissioned	Submarine Name & Number		Date Commissioned
Peto	SS 265	November 21, 1942	Sea Cat	SS 399	May 16, 1944
Pickerel*	SS 177	January 26, 1937	Sea Devil	SS 400	May 24, 1944
Picuda	SS 382	October 16, 1943	Sea Dog	SS 401	June 3, 1944
Pike	SS 173	December 2, 1935	Seadragon	SS 194	October 23, 1939
Pilotfish	SS 386	December 16, 1943	Sea Fox	SS 402	June 13, 1944
Pintado	SS 387	January 1, 1944	Seahorse	SS 304	March 31, 1943
Pipefish	SS 388	January 22, 1944	Seal	SS 183	April 30, 1938
Piper	SS 409	August 23, 1944	Sealion (1)*	SS 195	November 27, 1939
Piranha	SS 389	February 5, 1944	Sealion (2)	SS 315	March 8, 1944
Plaice	SS 390	February 12, 1944	Sea Owl	SS 405	July 17, 1944
Plunger	SS 179	November 19, 1936	Sea Poacher	SS 406	July 31, 1944
Pogy	SS 266	January 10, 1943	Searaven	SS 196	October 2, 1939
Pollack	SS 180	January 15, 1937	Sea Robin	SS 407	August 7, 1944
Pomfret	SS 391	February 19, 1944	Seawolf*	SS 197	December 1, 1939
Pompano*	SS 181	June 12, 1937	Segundo	SS 398	May 9, 1944
Pompon	SS 267	March 17, 1943	Sennet	SS 408	August 22, 1944
Porpoise	SS 172	August 15, 1935	Shad	SS 235	June 12, 1942
Puffer	SS 268	April 27, 1943	Shark*	SS 174	January 25, 1936
Queenfish	SS 393	March 11, 1944	Shark II*	SS 314	February 14, 1944
Quillback	SS 424	December 29, 1944	Silversides	SS 236	December 15, 1941
R-12*	SS 89	September 23, 1919	Skate	SS 305	April 15, 1943
Rasher	SS 269	June 8, 1943	Skipjack	SS 184	June 30, 1938
Raton	SS 270	July 13, 1943	Snapper	SS 185	December 15, 1937
Ray	SS 271	July 27, 1943	Snook*	SS 279	October 24, 1942
Razorback	SS 394	April 3, 1944	Spadefish	SS 411	March 9, 1944
Redfin	SS 272	August 31, 1943	Spearfish	SS 190	July 19, 1939
Redfish	SS 395	April 12, 1944	Spikefish	SS 404	June 30, 1944
Requin	SS 481	April 28, 1945	Spot	SS 413	August 3, 1944
Robalo*	SS 273	September 28, 1943	Springer	SS 414	October 18, 1944
Rock	SS 274	October 26, 1943	Steelhead	SS 280	December 7, 1942
Ronquil	SS 396	April 22, 1944	Sterlet	SS 392	March 4, 1944
Runner*	SS 275	July 30, 1942	Stickleback	SS 415	March 29, 1945
Runner II	SS 476	February 6, 1945	Stingray	SS 186	March 15, 1938
S-18	SS 123	April 3, 1924	Sturgeon	SS 187	June 25, 1938
S-23	SS 128	October 30, 1923	Sunfish	SS 281	July 15, 1942
S-26*	SS 131	October 15, 1923	Swordfish*	SS 193	July 22, 1939
S-27*	SS 132	January 22, 1924	Tambor	SS 198	June 3, 1940
S-28*	SS 133	December 13, 1923	Tang*	SS 306	October 15, 1943
S-30	SS 135	October 29, 1920	Tarpon	SS 175	March 12, 1936
S-31	SS 136	March 8, 1923	Tautog	SS 199	July 3, 1940
S-32	SS 137	February 21, 1923	Tench	SS 417	October 6, 1944
S-33	SS 138	December 21, 1922	Thornback	SS 418	October 13, 1944
S-34	SS 139	April 23, 1923	Threadfin	SS 410	August 30, 1944
S-35	SS 140	May 7, 1923	Thresher	SS 200	August 27, 1940
S-36*	SS 141	April 4, 1923	Tigrone	SS 419	October 25, 1944
S-37	SS 142	July 16, 1923	Tilefish	SS 307	December 15, 1943
S-38	SS 143	May 11, 1923	Tinosa	SS 283	January 15, 1943
S-39*	SS 144	September 14, 1923	Tirante	SS 420	November 6, 1944
S-40	SS 145	November 20, 1923	Toro	SS 422	December 8, 1944
S-41	SS 146	January 15, 1924	Torsk	SS 423	December 16, 1944
S-42	SS 153	November 20, 1924	Trepang	SS 412	May 22, 1944
S-43	SS 154	December 31, 1924	Trigger*	SS 237	January 31, 1942
S-44*	SS 155	February 16, 1925	Triton*	SS 201	August 15, 1940
S-45	SS 156	March 31, 1925	Trout*	SS 202	November 15, 1940
S-46	SS 157	June 5, 1925	Trutta	SS 421	November 16, 1944
S-47	SS 158	September 16, 1925	Tullibee*	SS 284	February 15, 1943
Sailfish	SS 192	May 15, 1940	Tuna	SS 203	January 2, 1941
Salmon	SS 182	March 15, 1938	Tunny	SS 282	September 1, 1942
Sandlance	SS 381	October 9, 1943	Wahoo*	SS 238	May 15, 1942
Sargo	SS 188	February 7, 1939	Whale	SS 239	June 1, 1942
Saury	SS 189	April 3, 1939			
Sawfish	SS 276	August 26, 1942			
Scabbardfish	SS 397	April 29, 1944			
Scamp*	SS 277	September 18, 1942			
Scorpion*	SS 278	October 1, 1942			
Sculpin*	SS 191	January 16, 1939			

* lost in action during World War II

147

Museums and Memorials

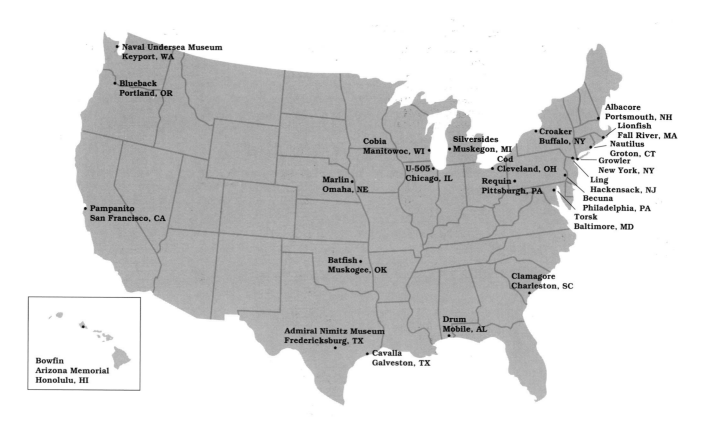

Admiral Nimitz Museum State Historical Park

340 E. Main
Fredericksburg, TX 78624

The Admiral Nimitz Museum honors the memory of World War II Pacific Fleet Admiral Chester A. Nimitz. The museum has 24,000 square feet of indoor exhibits and three acres of outdoor exhibits. Indoor displays cover the entire history of the Pacific war, using maps, photographs, models, and multimedia. The museum also features one of the Japanese midget submarines captured in the Pearl Harbor attack.

USS *Albacore*
Port of Portsmouth Maritime Museum & *Albacore* Park

600 Market Street
Portsmouth, NH 03801

The Navy built *Albacore* in 1953 with an innovative teardrop hull design. Today visitors can tour the 205-foot-long submarine and see this important bridge between the World War II fleet boat and the modern atomic submarine. In addition to the *Albacore*, the park includes a visitor center and memorial garden.

Arizona Memorial Museum

#1 Arizona Memorial Place
Honolulu, HI 96818

The *Arizona* Memorial Museum commemorates the Pearl Harbor attack of December 7, 1941, the "day of infamy." Located at Pearl Harbor on the Hawaiian island of Oahu, the museum consists of a visitor center run by the National Park Service and the USS *Arizona* Memorial. The memorial is a 184 foot white marble bridge that spans, but does not touch, the sunken hull of the battleship *Arizona*—destroyed in a magazine explosion during the Pearl Harbor raid. Visitors can tour the museum, watch a 20-minute documentary film on the Japanese attack, or browse the bookstore before taking a navy shuttle boat to the memorial, which lies in the harbor just off Ford Island.

USS *Batfish*
Muskogee War Memorial Park and Military Museum

P.O. Box 253
Muskogee, OK 74402

The memorial park is the site of the USS *Batfish*, a World War II fleet submarine. *Batfish* achieved fame by sinking three Japanese subs off the Philippines in February 1945. Visitors can tour the *Batfish* and adjacent interpretive museum. Batfish Park also has bronze stands to commemorate each of the 52 submarines lost during World War II and includes a special monument to the lost submarine, *Shark*.

USS Becuna
Cruiser Olympia Association
Penn's Landing
Del Ave & Spruce St.
Philadelphia, PA 19106

The World War II fleet submarine, *Becuna*, sits at Penn's landing on the Delaware River. Commissioned in 1944, *Becuna* made five war patrols and received four battle stars and a Presidential Unit citation. Visitors can tour *Becuna* and the adjacent historic cruiser, *Olympia*, which served as Admiral Dewey's flagship at the Battle of Manila Bay in 1898.

USS Blueback
Oregon Museum of Science & Industry
1945 SE Water Ave.
Portland, OR 97214

The *Blueback* was a modern, diesel-electric attack submarine when launched in 1959. The Oregon Museum of Science and Industry in Portland acquired the decommissioned *Blueback* from the Navy in 1994 and opened it to the public. In addition to the submarine, visitors can tour the extensive science museum.

USS Bowfin
USS Bowfin Submarine Museum and Park
11 Arizona Memorial Dr.
Honolulu, HI 96818

The museum features the World War II submarine, *Bowfin*, which conducted nine war patrols and sank many enemy ships. Also on display are photographs, models, plaques, weapon systems, uniforms, and artifacts which illustrate the history of the U.S. submarine service from the first attempt to use a submersible in warfare in 1776 to modern nuclear subs. Visitors can tour *Bowfin*, the museum, and the waterfront memorial park, which honors American submarines lost in World War II.

USS Cavalla
Seawolf Park
Moody Civic Center
21st St. & Beach Blvd.
Galveston, TX 77550

The World War II submarine, USS *Cavalla*, is open to the public at Seawolf Park in Galveston. In June 1944 *Cavalla* sank *Shokaku*, one of the Japanese aircraft carriers involved in the Pearl Harbor attack. Seawolf Park, named in honor the famous lost World War II sub, *Seawolf*, is also the site of the destroyer escort, USS *Stewart*.

USS Clamagore
Patriots Point Naval and Maritime Museum
40 Patriots Point Rd.
Mount Pleasant, SC 29464

The submarine, USS *Clamagore* on display in Charleston Harbor, was commissioned in 1945. *Clamagore* served in the Atlantic in the 1950s and 60s and was one of the U.S. Navy's last diesel subs. Attractions include the submarine, the World War II aircraft carrier, *Yorktown*, the destroyer, *Laffey*, the nuclear merchant ship, *Savannah*, and the Coast Guard cutter, *Ingham*. From Patriot's Point, tour boats also leave for Fort Sumter and for trips around Charleston Harbor and Naval Base.

USS Cobia
Wisconsin Maritime Museum
75 Maritime Dr.
Manitowoc, WI 54220

The submarine, USS *Cobia*, is moored next to the Wisconsin Maritime Museum in Manitowoc. *Cobia* was one of 28 submarines built at the Manitowoc shipyard during World War II. The museum covers Great Lakes maritime history and features a model ship gallery of sail and steam vessels. *Cobia* is maintained as it was during World War II and is open to the public.

USS Cod
1089 East 9th St.
Cleveland, OH 44114

Located at the waterfront between North Coast Harbor and Burke Lakefront Airport in Cleveland, USS *Cod* is a completely restored World War II U.S. submarine. Its interior remains largely as it was when *Cod* made its seventh and final war patrol against Japan in August 1945. The USS *Cod* site also houses on-shore displays of submarine apparatus, including a Mark 14 torpedo and other naval weaponry.

USS Croaker
Buffalo & Erie County Naval & Servicemen's Park
1 Naval Park Cove
Buffalo, NY 14202

Commissioned in 1944 the submarine, *Croaker*, served in the Pacific and sank the Japanese light cruiser, *Nagara*, and numerous merchant ships. *Croaker* is now part Buffalo and Erie County Naval and Servicemen's Park, which in addition to the submarine, includes the historic World War II destroyer, USS *The Sullivans*, the guided missile cruiser, USS *Little Rock*, an Air Force F-101 fighter interceptor jet, and a military museum, displaying artifacts of all branches of the armed services.

USS Drum
Battleship Memorial Park
P.O. Box 65
Mobile, AL 36601

The U.S. submarine, *Drum*, conducted 13 war patrols in the Pacific and sank numerous Japanese ships during World War II. The Navy donated *Drum* to Battleship Park in Mobile in 1969. In addition to touring *Drum*, visitors can go aboard the battleship, USS *Alabama*, or walk through the many military exhibits in the 100 acre park.

USS *Growler*
Intrepid Sea•Air•Space Museum
Intrepid Square
West 46th St. and 12th Ave.
New York, NY 10036

USS *Growler* is the world's only guided missile submarine open to the public. The *Growler* was armed with the Regulus missile, an early form of submarine-launched strategic weapons. In addition to *Growler*, visitors can tour the famous World War II aircraft carrier, *Intrepid*, the destroyer, *Edson*, and the sea, air and space museum.

USS *Ling*
New Jersey Naval Museum
P.O. Box 395
Hackensack, NJ 07602

The submarine, *Ling*, moored at Borg Park on the Hackensack River was launched in the last months of World War II and completed one patrol in the Atlantic before the surrender. The submarine memorial association restored *Ling* and opened it to the public in 1973.

USS *Lionfish*
Battleship Cove
Fall River, MA 02721

The Navy sent the submarine *Lionfish* into the Pacific in 1945 for three patrols. After many years of reserve status *Lionfish* became part of Battleship Cove in Fall River in 1972. Also at the site is the battleship, *Massachusetts*, and the destroyer, *Joseph P. Kennedy, Jr.*

USS *Marlin*
Freedom Park
2497 Freedom Park Rd.
Omaha, NE 68110

The *Marlin* was a small experimental coastal type submarine built in 1952 and used by the Navy for antisubmarine and mine warfare training until 1973. Visitors to Freedom Park can tour

the 131-foot-long submarine and the adjacent World War II minesweeper, USS *Hazard*.

Naval Undersea Museum
610 Dowell Street
Keyport, WA 98345

The museum covers the ocean environment with a variety of educational exhibits and the history of the U.S. Navy's operations in the ocean's depths. Also on display are underwater research vehicles such as *Trieste II* which has descended to the deepest part of the ocean.

USS *Nautilus*
Nautilus Memorial
Box 571
Crystal Lake Rd.
Groton, CT 06349-5000

The world's first atomic-powered submarine, the *Nautilus*, is part of the U.S. Navy's Submarine Force Library and Museum in Groton. The adjacent display area features a 50-foot cutaway model of the submarine, *Gato*, a full-size model of the *Turtle*, the Revolutionary War submersible, and two mini-theaters with films on submarines.

USS *Pampanito*
National Maritime Museum Assn.
Presidio of San Francisco
Building 275, Crissy Field
San Francisco, CA 94129

USS *Pampanito* is part of the National Maritime Museum Association. The submarine is berthed at Pier 45 Fisherman's Wharf in San Francisco Bay. It has been carefully restored to its World War II condition and is open to the public with a self-guided audio tour.

USS *Requin*
Carnegie Science Center
One Allegheny Ave.
Pittsburgh, PA 15212

Commissioned at the end of World War II, *Requin* was the U.S. Navy's

first radar picket submarine. The submarine became part of the Carnegie Science Center in 1990. The museum includes an Omnimax theater and extensive science exhibits.

USS *Silversides*
& Maritime Museum
1346 Bluff St.
Muskegon, MI 49441

Commissioned only eight days after the attack on Pearl Harbor in December 1941, *Silversides* conducted 14 war patrols in the Pacific and sank numerous Japanese ships. After serving as a reserve boat the submarine became the centerpiece of the USS *Silversides* & Maritime Museum at Muskegon in 1987.

USS *Torsk*
Baltimore Maritime Museum
Pier 3, Pratt Street
Baltimore, M.D. 21202

Launched in 1944, *Torsk* had the distinction of sinking the last two Japanese ships of World War II on August 14, 1945. *Torsk* served in the post-war Navy before the Baltimore Maritime Museum acquired it. Also on exhibit is the historic coast guard cutter, *Roger B. Taney*, and the lightship, *Chesapeake*.

German *U-505*
Museum of Science and Industry
57th Street and Lake Shore Dr.
Chicago, IL 60637

For people interested in seeing a foreign submarine, the Museum of Science and Industry offers the unique exhibit of a captured World War II German sub, the *U-505*. The U-boat sank eight Allied ships during the war before an American Naval task force captured it in June of 1944. A self-guided tour takes visitors through the sub's five main compartments. The museum also features a section on Navy technology at sea.

Bibliography

This bibliography includes books consulted in the preparation of *U.S. Submarines in World War II: An Illustrated History,* as well as titles that may be of further interest to the reader.

Alden, John D.:
The Fleet Submarine in the U.S. Navy: a Design and Construction History. Annapolis: United States Naval Institute, 1979.
U.S. Submarine Attacks During World War II. Annapolis: Naval Institute Press, 1989.

Allbury, A. G. *Bamboo and Bushido.* London: Robert Hale Limited, 1955.

Beach, Edward L. *Submarine!* New York: Henry Holt and Co., 1952.

Blair, Clay, Jr. *Silent Victory: the U.S. Submarine War Against Japan.* Philadelphia: J.B. Lippincott Co.,1975.

Blair, Joan and Clay Blair, Jr. *Return from the River Kwai.* New York: Simon and Schuster, 1979.

Bureau of Naval Personnel, ed.:
The Fleet Type Submarine. Washington, D.C.: United States Government Printing Office, 1946.
Naval Ordnance and Gunnery. Washington, D.C.: Unites States Government Printing Office, 1952.

Carpenter, Dorr and Norman Polmar. *Submarine of the Imperial Japanese Navy.* Annapolis: Naval Institute Press, 1986.

Cohen, Jerome B. *Japan's Economy in War and Reconstruction.* Minneapolis: University of Minnesota Press, 1949.

Costello, John. *The Pacific War 1941–1945.* New York: William Morrow and Company, Inc., 1981.

Crowl, Philip A. *Campaign in the Marianas.* Washington, D.C.: Department of the Army, Office of the Chief of Military History, 1960.

Dull, Paul S. *A Battle History of the Imperial Japanese Navy (1941–1945).* Annapolis: Naval Institute Press, 1978.

Drea, Edward J. *MacArthur's ULTRA Codebreaking and the War Against Japan, 1942–1945.* Lawrence: University of Kansas Press, 1992.

Enright, Joseph F. *Shinano!: the Sinking of Japan's Secret Supership.* New York: St. Martin's Press, 1987.

Farago, Ladislas. *The Broken Seal: The Story of "Operation Magic" and the Pearl Harbor Disaster.* New York: Random House, 1967.

Frank, Gerold and James D. Horan, with J.M. Eckberg. *U.S.S. Seawolf: Submarine Raider of the Pacific.* New York: G.P. Putnam's Sons, 1945.

Frank, Richard B. *Guadalcanal: the Definitive Account of the Landmark Battle.* New York: Random House, 1990.

Galantin, I. J. *Take Her Deep!* New York: Pocket Books, 1988.

Gates, P. J. and N. M. Lynn. *Ships, Submarines and the Sea.* London: Brassey's (UK) Ltd., 1990.

Gray, Edwyn. *The Devil's Device: Robert Whitehead and the History of the Torpedo.* Annapolis: Naval Institute Press, 1991.

Gugliotta, Bobette. *Pigboat 39: an American sub goes to war.* Lexington: University Press of Kentucky, 1984.

Holmes, W. J.:
Double-edged Secrets: U.S. Naval Intelligence Operations in the Pacific during World War II. Annapolis: Naval Institute Press, 1979.
Undersea Victory: The Influence of Submarine Operations on the War in the Pacific. Garden City, New York: Doubleday & Company, Inc., 1966

Jentschura, Hansgeorg, Dieter Jung, and Peter Mickel. Translated by Antony Preston and J.D. Brown. *Warships of the Imperial Japanese Navy, 1869–1945.* Annapolis: Naval Institute Press, 1977.

Jolie, E. W. *Brief History of U.S. Navy Torpedo Development.* Newport: Naval Underwater Systems Center, 1978.

Kahn, David. *The Codebreakers: The Story of Secret Writing.* London: Weidenfeld and Nicolson, 1967.

Kimmett, Larry and Margaret Regis. *The Attack on Pearl Harbor: An Illustrated History.* Seattle: Navigator Publishing, 1992.

Layton, Edwin T., with Roger Pineau and John Costello. *"And I was There." Pearl Harbor and Midway— Breaking the Secrets.* New York: William Morrow and Company, Inc., 1985.

Lockwood, Charles A. and Hans Christian Adamson. *Through Hell and Deep Water.* New York: Greenberg : Publisher, 1956.

Mendenhall, Corwin. *Submarine Diary.* Chapel Hill, North Carolina: Algon-quin Books of Chapel Hill, 1991.

Miller, Edward S. *War Plan Orange: the U.S. Strategy to Defeat Japan 1897–1945.* Annapolis: United States Naval Institute, 1991.

Miller, John, Jr. *Guadalcanal: The First Offensive..* Washington, D.C.: Department of the Army, Historical Division, 1949.

Morison, Samuel Eliot. *The Rising Sun in the Pacific. History of the United States Naval Operations in World War II, vol. 3.* Boston: Little, Brown and Co., 1948.

Office of the Chief of Naval Operations, ed. *O.N.I. 208-J Japanese Merchant Ship Recognition Manual.* Washington, D.C.: United States Navy, 1942.

O'Kane, Richard H.:
Clear the Bridge: the War Patrols of U.S.S. Tang. New York: Bantam Books, 1981.
Wahoo. Novato, California: Presidio Press, 1987.

Polmar, Norman. *The American Submarine.* Annapolis: Nautical and Aviation Publishing Company of America, 1981.

Roscoe, Theodore. *United States Submarine Operations in World War II.* Annapolis: United States Naval Institute, 1949.

Schratz, Paul R. *Submarine Commander: A Story of World War II and Korea.* Lexington: University Press of Kentucky, 1988.

Smith, S. E., ed. *The United States Navy in World War II.* New York: William Morrow & Co., Inc. 1966.

Spector, Ronald H. *Eagle Against the Sun..* New York: The Free Press, 1985.

Stewart, William H. *Ghost Fleet of the Truk Lagoon.* Missoula, Montana: Pictorial Histories Publishing Co., 1986.

Toland, John. *The Rising Sun: the Decline and Fall of the Japanese Empire.* New York: Random House, 1970.

Underbrink, Robert L. *Destination Corregidor.* Annapolis: United States Naval Institute, 1971.

United States Division of Naval Intelligence, ed. *Japanese Naval Vessels of World War II.* Annapolis: Naval Institute Press, 1987.

United States Strategic Bombing Survey, ed.:
The Campaigns of the Pacific War. Washington, D.C.: United States Government Printing Office, 1946.
The Offensive Mine Laying Campaign Against Japan. Washington, D.C.: Department of the Navy, Headquarters Naval Material Command, 1969.

Van der Vat, Dan. *The Pacific Campaign: World War II, The U.S.-Japanese Naval War, 1941–1945..* New York: Simon & Schuster, 1991.

Watts, Anthony J., and Brian G. Gordon. *The Imperial Japanese Navy.* Garden City, New York: Doubleday and Co., 1971.

Westwood, J. N. *Fighting Ships of World War II.* London: Sidgwick & Jackson, 1975.

Wheeler, Keith. *War Under the Pacific.* Alexandria: Time-Life Books, 1981.

Whitley, M. J. *Destroyers of World War Two.* Annapolis: Naval Institute Press, 1988.

Zich, Arthur. *The Rising Sun.* Alexandria, Virginia: Time-Life Books, 1977.

Picture Credits

Cover: National Archives

Front Matter: 6—courtesy, Paul Farace, USS *Cod*. 9—National Archives.

Japanese Empire: 10—National Archives. 11—National Archives.

Two Plans: 12—National Archives. 13—National Archives.

Early U.S. Submarines: 14—Naval Historical Center.

Fleet Submarine: 16–17—courtesy, Russell Booth, The National Maritime Museum Association. 17—(top) courtesy, Paul Farace, USS *Cod*. 18—courtesy, Paul Farace, USS *Cod*. 19—courtesy, Paul Farace, USS *Cod*.

Aboard the Boat: 20—(top) National Archives, (center) USS *Bowfin* Museum. 21—National Archives.

Pearl Harbor: 22—National Archives. 23—National Archives.

First Empire Patrol: 24—National Archives. 25—Imperial War Museum.

Philippines Disaster/Cavite: 27—National Archives.

Philippines Disaster/Lingayen Gulf: 28—Naval Historical Center.

Torpedo Failure: 30—U.S. Navy. 31—(top) U.S. Navy, (bottom) National Archives.

Invasion of the Dutch East Indies: 33—(top) Naval Historical Center, (bottom) National Archives.

Withdrawal to Australia: 34—National Archives. 35—National Archives.

Destination Corregidor: 36—National Archives. 37—National Archives.

Unrestricted Submarine Warfare: 38—National Archives. 39—Naval Historical Center.

A Vulnerable Empire: 40—U.S. Navy.

ULTRA—The Secret Weapon: 42—(center) Naval Historical Center, (bottom) National Security Agency. 43—Naval Historical Center.

Midway: 44—National Archives. 45—National Archives.

War in the Aleutians: 46—National Archives. 47—National Archives.

Guadalcanal: 48—National Archives.

Makin Raid: 51—(top) National Archives, (bottom) Naval Historical Center.

The Emperor's Front Door: 52—National Archives. 53—National Archives.

Minelaying: 55—(top) National Archives, (bottom) USS *Bowfin* Museum.

Silversides: 56—National Archives. 57—National Archives.

January 1943: 58—National Archives. 59—(top) National Archives, (bottom) Naval Historical Center.

Reinforcements: 60—National Archives. 61—National Archives.

Take Her Down: 63—(top) courtesy, William Soczek, (bottom) Naval Historical Center.

Wahoo: 64—National Archives. 65—National Archives.

The Yellow Sea: 67—National Archives.

Depth Charged!: 68—National Archives. 69—U.S. Navy.

Solemn Victory: 70—National Archives. 71—National Archives.

New Weapons: 72—U.S. Navy. 73—USS *Bowfin* Museum.

Wahoo's Last Patrol: 75—Naval Historical Center.

Into the East China Sea: 76—U.S. Navy. 77—Naval Historical Center.

Bowfin: 78—National Archives. 79—USS *Bowfin* Museum.

Invasion of the Gilbert Islands: 80—National Archives.

Medal of Honor: 82—(center) Naval Historical Center, (bottom) National Archives.

Sister Ships: 84—National Archives. 85—courtesy, George Rocek.

The Grand Escort Force: 86—Smithsonian Institution.

January 1944: 88—National Archives. 89—National Archives.

Invasion of the Marshall Islands: 90—National Archives. 91—Naval Historical Center.

Raid on Truk: 92—National Archives.

Lifeguard Duty: 94—USS *Bowfin* Museum. 95—National Archives.

Japan's Vital Artery: 96—National Archives.

Bamboo Convoy No. 1: 98—National Archives.

Harder: 100—USS *Bowfin* Museum. 101—National Archives.

Invasion of the Marianas: 103—National Archives.

Battle of the Philippine Sea: 104—(top) National Archives, (bottom) USS *Bowfin* Museum. 105—Imperial War Museum.

Convoy College: 107—National Archives.

Loss of Harder: 108—National Archives. 109—National Archives.

Survivors of the River Kwai: 110—National Archives. 111—(top) U.S. Navy, (bottom) Naval Historical Center. 112—National Archives. 113—National Archives.

Seawolf's Last Run: 114—USS *Bowfin* Museum. 115—National Archives.

Battle of Leyte Gulf: 116—National Archives. 117—Naval Historical Center.

The Biggest Carrier: 120—USS *Bowfin* Museum.

Flasher: 123—National Archives.

January 1945: 124—National Archives.

Into the Sea of Japan: 126—USS *Bowfin* Museum.

Silent Hunter: 128—National Archives. 129—National Archives.

The Final Attack: 130—courtesy, Ervin Schmidt. 131—courtesy, Ervin Schmidt.

Deck of the Missouri: 132—National Archives. 133—National Archives.

The Enlisted Men: 134—National Archives. 135—(top) courtesy, William Soczek, (bottom) National Archives. 136—courtesy, Charles Stewart. 137—(top) courtesy, Tudor Davis, (bottom) National Archives. 138—(top) courtesy, John Fankhauser. 139—courtesy, the Naze Family. 140—(top) courtesy, Ralph Van Horn, (bottom) U.S. Navy. 141—(top) courtesy, Pete Mitchell, (bottom) National Archives. 142—courtesy, Joe Phenneger. 143—(top) courtesy, Ervin Schmidt, (bottom) National Archives.

Index

154

158

From the authors of *U.S. Submarines in World War II* . . .

THE ATTACK ON PEARL HARBOR
An Illustrated History

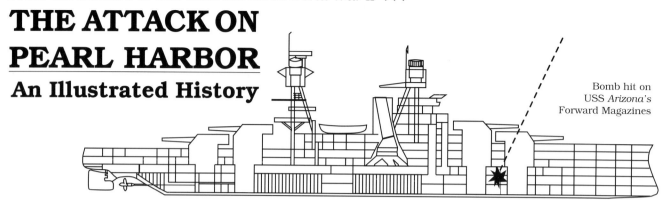

Bomb hit on USS *Arizona's* Forward Magazines

For the first time "The Day of Infamy" is recreated in stunning detail. Each phase of the battle is carefully analyzed with maps, photos, and unique graphics. From the early stages of Japanese planning through the destruction of Battleship Row to the remarkable salvage of the U.S. Pacific Fleet, the *Illustrated History* gives a front-row seat to the attack that brought the United States into World War II. 128 pages; over 200 illustrations.

"No matter how many books you've read about the Japanese attack . . . *The Attack on Pearl Harbor: An Illustrated History* will add to your understanding of the events that morning."
—*The Charleston Gazette*

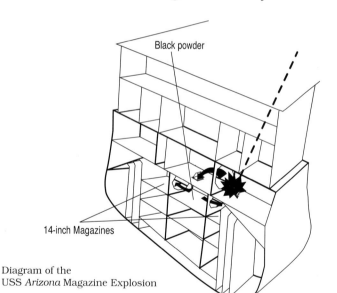

Black powder

14-inch Magazines

Diagram of the
USS *Arizona* Magazine Explosion

Includes:

- Causes of War
- The Plan
- The Target
- The Weapon
- Early Warnings
- Tora, Tora, Tora
- Torpedo Attack
- High-Level Bombing
- Loss of USS *Arizona*
- Assault on the Air Bases
- Midget Submarine Attack
- Final Action
- Declaration of War
- Fate of the Commanders
- Survivors' Tales

"Brilliant! The Best Illustrated Book on the Pearl Harbor Attack!"